Enrich Book

Grade

MW00949224

PROVIDES Daily Enrichment Activities

 HOUGHTON MIFFLIN HARCOURT

Printed in the U.S.A.

ISBN 978-0-547-39223-3

3 4 5 6 7 8 9   2266   19 18 17 16 15

4500558487   ^ B C D E

Table of Contents

BIG IDEA 2: Ratio, Proportional Reasoning, and Percent

Chapter 5: Ratios, Rates, and Percents

Chapter 6: Units of Measure

Chapter 7: Collect, Organize, and Analyze Data

Chapter 8: Probability

BIG IDEA 3: Expressions, Equations, and Functions

Chapter 9: Integers

Chapter 10: Algebra: Equations and Functions

Chapter 11: Measurement

Chapter 12: Perimeter and Area

Chapter 13: Surface Area and Volume

Name _____

Break the Exponent Bricks

**Fill in the missing number to complete the number sentence.
Shade or cross out the answer in the bricks below to find the
route from the left to the right.**

1. $3^{\underline{\quad}} = 2{,}187$	**2.** $5^{\underline{\quad}} = 1$	**3.** $6^{\underline{\quad}} = 1{,}296$
4. $2^{\underline{\quad}} = 256$	**5.** $4^{\underline{\quad}} = 4{,}096$	**6.** $\underline{\quad}^{1} = 9$
7. $2^{9} = \underline{\quad\quad}$	**8.** $\underline{\quad}^{2} = 64$	**9.** $7^{\underline{\quad}} = 343$
10. $1^{13} = \underline{\quad\quad}$	**11.** $5^{\underline{\quad}} = 3{,}125$	**12.** $\underline{\quad}^{7} = 0$

Problem Number

	1	2	3	4	5	6	7	8	9	10	11	12
A	6	0	4	7	5	7	18	5	7	0	0	6
N	7	1	5	8	6	8	9	6	6	5	1	7
S	8	2	6	9	7	9	512	7	5	4	2	8
W	9	3	7	10	8	10	256	8	4	3	3	9
E	10	4	8	11	9	11	1,024	9	3	2	4	0
R	11	5	9	12	10	12	81	32	2	1	5	1

13. Stretch Your Thinking Write a number
sentence with an exponent where the
answer is one of the choices for Problem
7 that you did not cross out.

14. ⬛WRITE Math▶ Is 6^4 equal to 4^6? Explain
your answer.

_____

_____

_____

Name _____

Invisible Divisible

Use the clues to find all possibilities for the missing digit in each number.

1. The number below is divisible by 3.
What could be the missing digit?

298,[ ]11

_____

2. The number below is divisible by 4.
What could be the missing digit?

340,2[ ]6

_____

3. The number below is divisible by 5.
What could be the missing digit?

471,9[ ]5

_____

4. The number below is divisible by 9.
What could be the missing digit?

[ ]06,349

_____

5. The number below is divisible by 6.
What could be the missing digit?

427,71[ ]

_____

6. The number below is divisible by 3 and 9.
What could be the missing digit?

9,864,[ ]28

_____

7. The number below is divisible by 4 and 6.
What could be the missing digit?

7,302,6[ ]4

_____

8. The number below is divisible by 2 and 9.
What could be the missing digit?

1[ ],545,266

_____

9. Stretch Your Thinking A number is divisible by 2 if the last digit is
divisible by 2. A number is divisible by 4 if the last two digits form a
number divisible by 4. A number is divisible by 8 if the last three digits
form a number divisible by 8. Find a possible pattern. Use this pattern
to describe a divisibility rule for 16. Test your rule on each of the
following numbers.

383,488   295,614   314,320   583,052

_____

_____

_____

Symmetric Factor Trees

Both factor trees show the prime factorization of 40. The factor tree
on the right is symmetrical because the first two factors branch out
so all the prime factors are on a horizontal line.

"Not Symmetric" underneath.

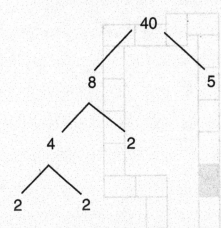

"Symmetric" underneath.

Create a symmetric factor tree for each number.

1. 90

2. 16

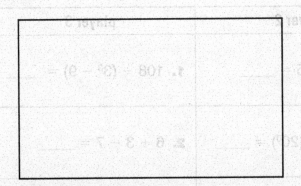

3. Stretch Your Thinking Create a
symmetric factor tree for a number that
has more than two prime factors and is
greater than 100.

4. [WRITE Math] Can you make a symmetric
factor tree for every composite number?
Explain.

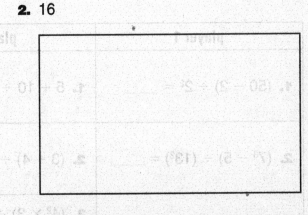

_____

_____

_____

Order of Operations Game

Three players are playing a board game. Complete the expressions
below and move the player's piece the same number of spaces as
the answer for the expression. Do not count the start space.

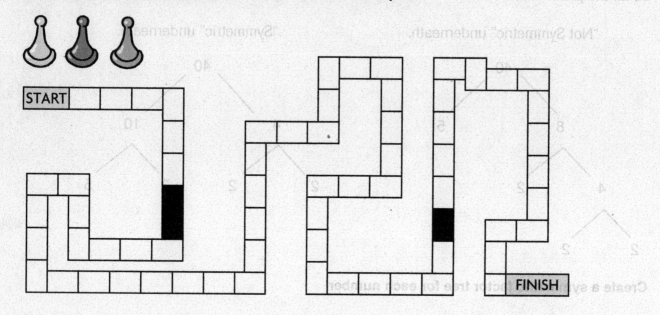

player 1	player 2	player 3
1. $(50 - 2) \div 2^2 =$ ____	**1.** $5 + 10 \div 5 =$ ____	**1.** $108 \div (3^3 - 9) =$ ____
2. $(7^3 - 5) \div (13^2) =$ ____	**2.** $(3 + 4) \div (20^0) =$ ____	**2.** $6 + 3 - 7 =$ ____
3. $(55 - 1^5) \div 9 =$ ____	**3.** $(4^2 \times 3) \div (2^2 \times 6)$ ____	**3.** $(8^2 \div 16) \times (11 - 6)$ ____
4. $(15 - 6^2 \div 4) + (3^2 \times 2)$ = ____	**4.** $4^1 \times (8 + 51 \div 17)$ = ____	**4.** $12^2 - (10 + 4 \times 5^2)$ = ____

5. Stretch Your Thinking On his next move, player 1 is given
an expression that moves his game piece directly to the finish
space on the board. The expression has a division and a subtraction
operation and an exponent. Write a possible expression.

_____

Backward Numbers

Start with the known value and work backward to solve.

1. There is a jar of pencils on the table. There are 3 times as many red pencils as blue and 1 more green than red. There are 7 green pencils. How many blue pencils are there?

   _____

2. Mark, Jim, and Jose are shooting basketball free throws. Mark made twice as many free throws as Jim. Mark made 1 less free throw than Jose. Jose made 19 free throws. How many free throws did Jim make?

   _____

3. Susan, Tanisha, and Maria are neighbors. Susan is 2 years younger than Tanisha. Tanisha is 5 years older than Maria. Maria is 21. What is Susan's age?

   _____

4. Jessica has twice as much money as Keira. Keira has $5 more than Gita and Gita has $6 less than Jae Hyun. Jae Hyun has $11. How much money does Jessica have? How much money do they have altogether?

   _____

5. Multiply a number by 3, and add 7. Multiply the sum by 2, and you get 44. What is the number?

   _____

6. Divide a number by 12, and subtract 1. Multiply the difference by 8, and you get 32. What is the number?

   _____

WRITE Math ▷ Explain how to work backward to solve Exercises 1–6.

_____

_____

_____

_____

Find the Property Then Use the Property

The number sentences that follow can be completed using one of the properties below. Identify the sentence that can be solved using the property. Then complete the number sentence and write it below the property in the table.

Associative Property of Addition	Identity Property of 1
_____	_____
Associative Property of Multiplication	Commutative Property of Addition
_____	_____
Commutative Property of Multiplication	Distributive Property
_____	_____
Identity Property of 0	
_____	

$1 \times 17 =$ _____

_____ $\times 11 = 13 \times (8 \times 11)$

$9 \times (5 + 3) =$ _____ $+ (9 \times 3)$

_____ $+ 0 = 49$

_____ $\times 29 = 29 \times 3$

$(7 + 6) +$ _____ $= 7 + (6 + 25)$

$51 +$ _____ $= 39 + 51$

1. **Stretch Your Thinking** Write $4 \times (25 + 4)$ a different way using the Distributive Property. Then evaluate.

_____

2. **WRITE Math** Explain how the Associative Properties for Addition and Multiplication are alike.

_____

_____

Which Expression Am I?

Match each word expression on the left with the correct algebraic expression on the right.

a number decreased by 9	$4n - 15$
9 times the sum of a number and 4	$n^3 + n$
15 less than 4 times a number	$n - 9$
the cube of a number increased by the number	$9n$
the product of a number and 9	$n^2 + 7n$
the square of a number, increased by the product of 7 and the number	$9(n + 4)$
the quotient of a number and 9	$\dfrac{n}{9} + 4$
4 times a number, increased by 15	$15 - 4n$
4 more than a number divided by 9	$9 - n$
a number increased by 9	$4n + 15$
4 times a number less than 15	$\dfrac{n}{9}$
9 decreased by a number	$n + 9$

Round and Round They Go

Evaluate the expression for each value of *a*. Circle the correct answer.

$$8a - 2(3 + a)$$

6

70   (*a* = 2)   0

44

69

132   (*a* = 3)   48

12

414

30   (*a* = 6)   288

144

$$3(a - 1)^2 + 2$$

13

9   (*a* = 4)   29

123

3

7   (*a* = 2)   5

27

110

18   (*a* = 7)   402

22

$$5a - 3a + 11 - a^2$$

3

23   (*a* = 4)   35

7

2

3   (*a* = 3)   18

8

0

12   (*a* = 1)   17

5

Name _____

Expression Secret Code

Find equivalent expressions to break the code and solve the riddle.

Riddle: What did one math book say to the other math book?

$3x$	2	$9 - x$	$8x + 9$	$10x - 5$	9	$5x + 8$
A	**B**	**C**	**D**	**E**	**F**	**G**
$x + 1$	$17x$	$10x - 10$	13	$16x$	$2x$	$8x - 10$
H	**I**	**J**	**K**	**L**	**M**	**N**
$17 - 5x$	$5x - 12$	$5 - 10x$	$4x$	$7x$	$12 - 15x$	$6x + 15$
O	**P**	**Q**	**R**	**S**	**T**	**U**
$15x$	10	$6x$	$x - 7$	$5x$		
V	**W**	**X**	**Y**	**Z**		

$5x + 12x$ $3(3x + 2x)$ $2x - 5 + 8x$ $6x - x + 8$ $7 - 5x + 10$

___   ___   ___   ___   ___

$3(4 - 5x)$ $2x + 3x - 12$ $2x + 2x$ $8 + 9 - 5x$ $8x + 2 - 8x$

___   ___   ___   ___   ___

$4(x + 3x)$ $5x + 5x - 5$ $2x + (5x \cdot 0)$ $x + 4x + 2x$

___   ___   ___   ___!

Digit Logic

Find the missing numbers. Each symbol stands for a different
digit from 0–9. The dark dots represent decimal places.

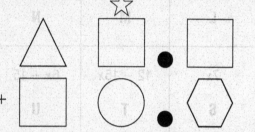

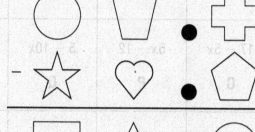

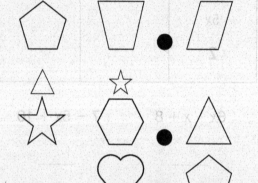

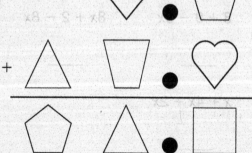

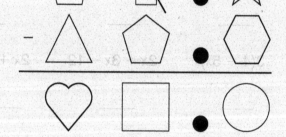

1. **Stretch Your Thinking** Create your own
   set of symbols for a subtraction problem
   with decimals. Show your answer.

   _____

Name That Product

**Write the multiplication problem and find the
product that each decimal square models.**

1.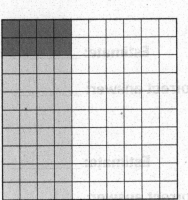

2.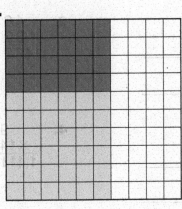

3.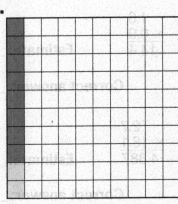

_____

4.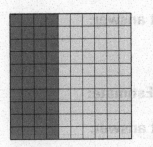

5.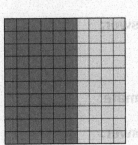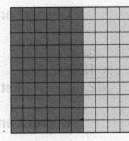

_____

_____

6. Stretch Your Thinking Create a
decimal square that models 0.75 × 0.65.
Then find the product.

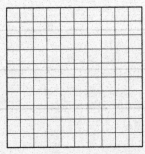

_____

7. ▐ WRITE Math ▶ Explain how the model
shows the product in problem 6.

_____

_____

_____

_____

_____

Name _____

Place the Decimal Point

Each answer shows the decimal point in the wrong place.
Estimate each product. Then make sure the decimal point is
put in the correct place.

1.
$$\begin{array}{r} 1.6 \\ \times\ 0.9 \\ \hline 14.4 \end{array}$$
Estimate: _____

Correct answer: _____

2.
$$\begin{array}{r} 4.6 \\ \times\ 3.2 \\ \hline 147.2 \end{array}$$
Estimate: _____

Correct answer: _____

3.
$$\begin{array}{r} 2.7 \\ \times\ 18.1 \\ \hline 4.887 \end{array}$$
Estimate: _____

Correct answer: _____

4.
$$\begin{array}{r} 9.6 \\ \times 14.7 \\ \hline 1,411.2 \end{array}$$
Estimate: _____

Correct answer: _____

5.
$$\begin{array}{r} 0.9 \\ \times\ 57.9 \\ \hline 5.211 \end{array}$$
Estimate: _____

Correct answer: _____

6.
$$\begin{array}{r} 0.75 \\ \times\ 4.22 \\ \hline 316.5 \end{array}$$
Estimate: _____

Correct answer: _____

7.
$$\begin{array}{r} 34.5 \\ \times\ 12.2 \\ \hline 42.09 \end{array}$$
Estimate: _____

Correct answer: _____

8.
$$\begin{array}{r} 28.8 \\ \times\ 15.5 \\ \hline 4.464 \end{array}$$
Estimate: _____

Correct answer: _____

WRITE Math How can estimating the product help you place the
decimal point?

_____

_____

_____

_____

_____

Name _____

Dazzling Division

Match each division problem with the correct model.

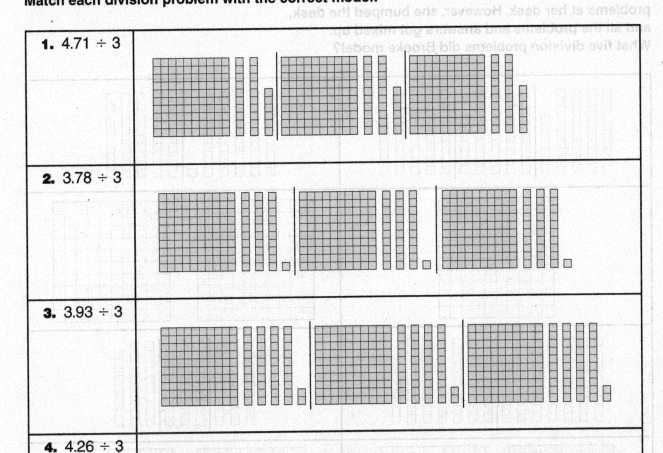

1. 4.71 ÷ 3	
2. 3.78 ÷ 3	
3. 3.93 ÷ 3	
4. 4.26 ÷ 3	

5. Stretch Your Thinking Describe how you could use decimal squares to model 0.05 ÷ 10.

_____

_____

_____

_____

6. Use the figure below to model 0.24 ÷ 4.

Division Puzzle Pieces

Brooke used decimal squares to model five division
problems at her desk. However, she bumped the desk,
and all the problems and answers got mixed up.
What five division problems did Brooke model?

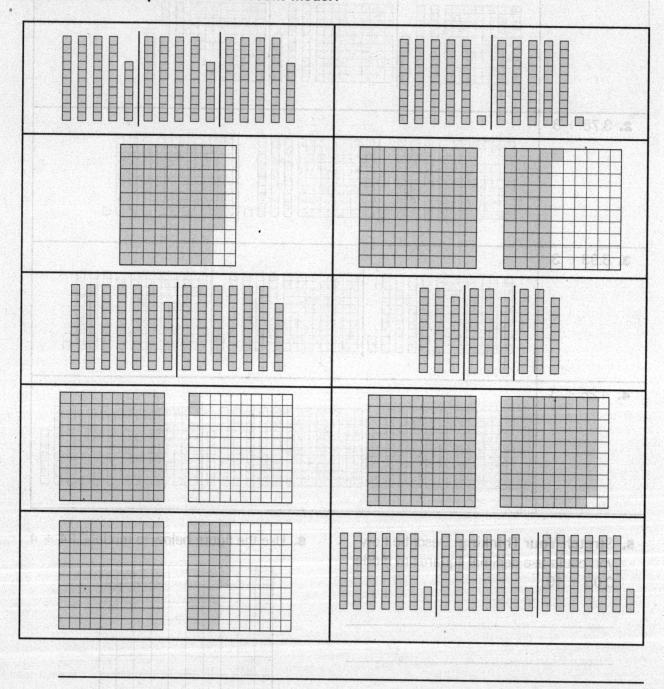

_____   _____

_____   _____

_____   _____

Find the Decimal Point

Circle the correct answer without actually dividing.

1. $3.45 \div 0.5 =$
6.9
0.69
0.069

2. $1.52 \div 0.08 =$
19
1.9
0.19

3. $1.08 \div 1.8 =$
6.0
0.6
0.06

4. $2.3 \div 0.23 =$
100
10
0.1

5. $0.009 \div 0.1 =$
9
0.9
0.09

6. $2.004 \div 0.02 =$
100.2
10.2
1.2

7. $30.6 \div 0.006 =$
51,000
5,100
510

8. $2.004 \div 0.0005 =$
4,008
408
48

9. $50.26 \div 2 =$
251.3
25.13
2.513

10. $0.00006 \div 0.3 =$
2
0.002
0.0002

11. $64.028 \div 0.4 =$
16,007
1,600.7
160.07

12. $4.1 \div 2.05 =$
20
2
0.2

13. $480.3 \div 0.03 =$
161,000
160,100
16,010

14. $5 \div 0.0001 =$
500,000
50,000
5,000

15. How many times should you move the decimal point in the dividend if the divisor is 0.000000009?

_____

16. Stretch Your Thinking If the dividend is a whole number and the divisor is 3.68, how do you move the decimal point for the dividend?

_____

_____

_____

Olympic Problems 50

Runners that hold Olympic records run at different rates because they run different distances. Usually, the longer the race, the slower the rate. The table shows the Olympic records for several races. In the table, 1:42.58 means 1 minute and 42.58 seconds.

Men's Olympic Records		
Race	Olympic Record Time (sec)	Year
100 meters	9.69	2008
200 meters	19.30	2008
400 meters	43.49	1996
800 meters	1:42.58	1996
1,500 meters	3:32.07	2000
5,000 meters	12:57.82	2008

Use the table to solve each problem. Round numbers to the nearest thousandth when necessary.

1. Usain Bolt from Jamaica was the Olympic record holder for the 100 meter and the 200 meter races in 2008. If he were able to run at the same rate as he did for the 100 meter race, how long would it take him to run 400 meters?

   _38.76_

2. In 2008, Kenenisa Bekele from Ethiopia was the Olympic record holder for the 5,000 meter race. If he ran at the same rate as he ran the 5,000 meter race, how long would it take him to run 100 meters?

   _3 g_

3. Vebjørn Rodal from Norway was the Olympic record holder for the 800 meter race in 1996. In 2008, his Olympic record still stood. At this pace, about how many meters could he run in 7.5 minutes?

   About 4000

4. In 2008, Kenenisa Bekele also held the Olympic record for the 10,000 meter race. He ran the 10,000 meter race in about 27 minutes 1 second. At this rate, how many seconds would it take Kenenisa to run 2 kilometers?

   _____

WRITE Math ▶ How can solving a simpler problem help you solve Problem 2?

_____

_____

_____

_____

_____

_____

Name _____

Repeat, Repeat, Repeat

Every fraction can be written as a terminating or repeating decimal by dividing the numerator by the denominator until the quotient terminates or starts repeating. Write a bar above the digit or digits that repeat.

Write each fraction as a repeating decimal.

1. $\frac{7}{9}$ 0.777	2. $\frac{2}{7}$ 0.285	3. $\frac{8}{11}$ 0.727
4. $\frac{2}{13}$ 0.153	5. $\frac{6}{7}$ 0.857	6. $\frac{3}{14}$ 0.214
7. $\frac{2}{6}$ 0.333	8. $\frac{8}{12}$ 0.666	9. $\frac{4}{9}$ 0.444

10. **Stretch Your Thinking** Write repeating decimals for the fractions $\frac{1}{11}$, $\frac{2}{11}$, and $\frac{3}{11}$. Find a pattern that you can use to write $\frac{4}{11}$ as a repeating decimal.

0.09 09
0.141
0.272
0.363

The first digit increase by one tenth every higher fraction.

11. **Stretch Your Thinking** Write repeating decimals for $\frac{1}{9}$, $\frac{1}{99}$, and $\frac{1}{999}$. What do you think is the repeating decimal for $\frac{1}{9,999}$?

0.11
0.01

Every time his higher it adds a zero in the tenths, hundreths, thousands etc.

the **Right Path**

th from $\frac{1}{4}$ to 3.1 in order from least to greatest.

Sta_____ and end at 3.1.

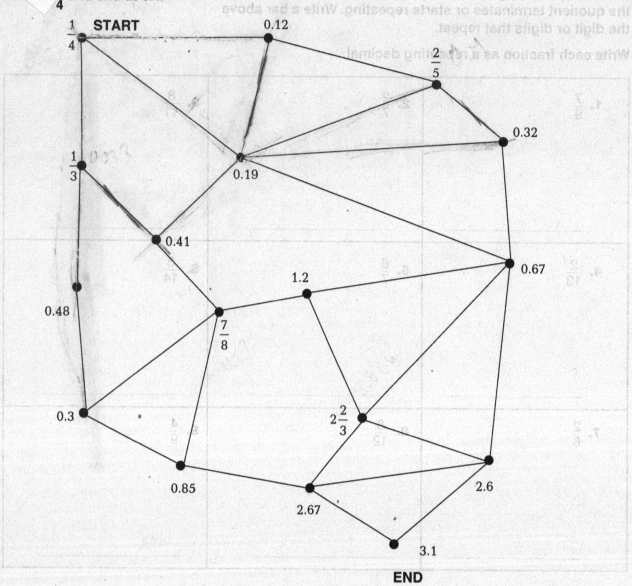

END

1. **Stretch Your Thinking** Find a different
   path through the maze by changing some
   of the numbers.

2. **WRITE Math** Explain how you found the
   answer to the problem you wrote.

_____

_____

_____

_____

Mix and Match

Lyle used fraction bars to do his math homework. He modeled
each problem using fraction bars but forgot to write which problem
he modeled. Help Lyle match each problem with the correct model.
Then write the answer.

1. $\frac{3}{5} + \frac{3}{10}$ F	**2.** $\frac{5}{8} + \frac{1}{4}$ C	**3.** $1 - \frac{2}{3}$ B	**4.** $\frac{7}{16} + \frac{3}{8}$ G
5. $2 - \frac{4}{5}$ D	**6.** $\frac{5}{6} + \frac{2}{3}$ A	**7.** $2 - \frac{3}{4}$ H	**8.** $\frac{7}{12} + \frac{1}{4}$ E

A.
| $\frac{1}{6}$ | $\frac{1}{6}$ | $\frac{1}{6}$ | $\frac{1}{6}$ | $\frac{1}{6}$ | $\frac{1}{3}$ | $\frac{1}{3}$ |
| 1 | | | $\frac{1}{2}$ | | | |

B.
| $\frac{1}{3}$ | $\frac{1}{3}$ | $\frac{1}{3}$ |

C.
| $\frac{1}{8}$ | $\frac{1}{8}$ | $\frac{1}{8}$ | $\frac{1}{8}$ | $\frac{1}{8}$ | $\frac{1}{4}$ |
| $\frac{1}{8}$ | $\frac{1}{8}$ | $\frac{1}{8}$ | $\frac{1}{8}$ | $\frac{1}{8}$ | $\frac{1}{8}$ |

D.
| 1 |
| $\frac{1}{5}$ | $\frac{1}{5}$ | $\frac{1}{5}$ | $\frac{1}{5}$ | $\frac{1}{5}$ |

E.
| $\frac{1}{12}$ | $\frac{1}{12}$ | $\frac{1}{12}$ | $\frac{1}{12}$ | $\frac{1}{12}$ | $\frac{1}{12}$ | $\frac{1}{12}$ | $\frac{1}{4}$ |
| $\frac{1}{6}$ | $\frac{1}{6}$ | $\frac{1}{6}$ | $\frac{1}{6}$ | $\frac{1}{6}$ |

F.
| $\frac{1}{5}$ | $\frac{1}{5}$ | $\frac{1}{5}$ | $\frac{1}{10}$ | $\frac{1}{10}$ | $\frac{1}{10}$ |
| $\frac{1}{10}$ | $\frac{1}{10}$ | $\frac{1}{10}$ | $\frac{1}{10}$ | $\frac{1}{10}$ | $\frac{1}{10}$ | $\frac{1}{10}$ | $\frac{1}{10}$ |

G.
| $\frac{1}{16}$ | $\frac{1}{16}$ | $\frac{1}{16}$ | $\frac{1}{16}$ | $\frac{1}{16}$ | $\frac{1}{16}$ | $\frac{1}{16}$ | $\frac{1}{8}$ | $\frac{1}{8}$ | $\frac{1}{8}$ |
| $\frac{1}{16}$ | $\frac{1}{16}$ | $\frac{1}{16}$ | $\frac{1}{16}$ | $\frac{1}{16}$ | $\frac{1}{16}$ | $\frac{1}{16}$ | $\frac{1}{16}$ | $\frac{1}{16}$ | $\frac{1}{16}$ | $\frac{1}{16}$ | $\frac{1}{16}$ | $\frac{1}{16}$ | $\frac{1}{16}$ |

H.
| 1 |
| $\frac{1}{4}$ | $\frac{1}{4}$ | $\frac{1}{4}$ | $\frac{1}{4}$ |

9. Stretch Your Thinking Explain why
you model $\frac{1}{2} + \frac{1}{4}$ with fraction bars that
are the same size.

You can model them
will the same bar
size because $\frac{1}{2}$ is $= \frac{2}{4}$.
Two-fourth is a two $\frac{1}{4}$
blocks.

10. WRITE Math ▸ Explain how you can tell
which models represent subtraction
problems.

It will boy the
number that is
being subtracted.

Plus or Minus Paths

Find the path whose answer is 17. Write the math expression for the path below.

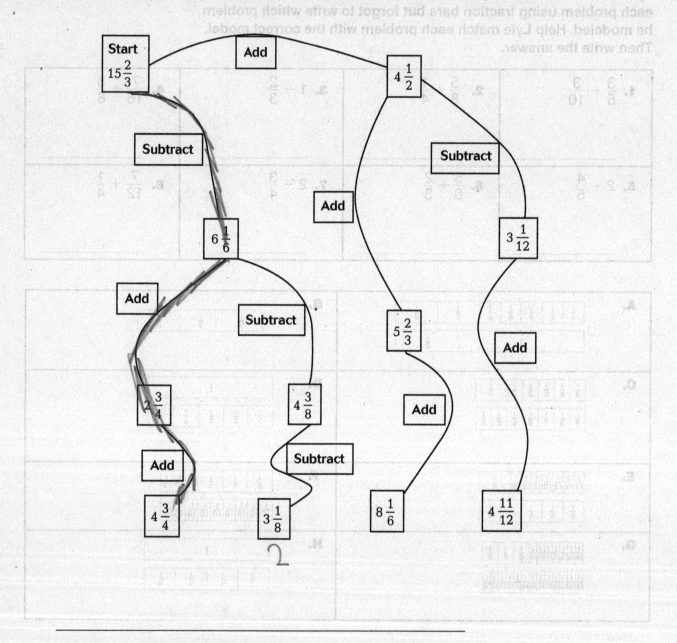

2

---

1. **Stretch Your Thinking** Select another path. Find the answer for that path.

The answer for my second path is 2.

2. **WRITE Math** Explain how you found the answer to the problem above.

I found my answer by subtracting and adding the numbers it said how to.

Star Ray Differences

Start in the center of the star. Subtract the fraction or mixed number along the arrows to find the five answers in simplest form.

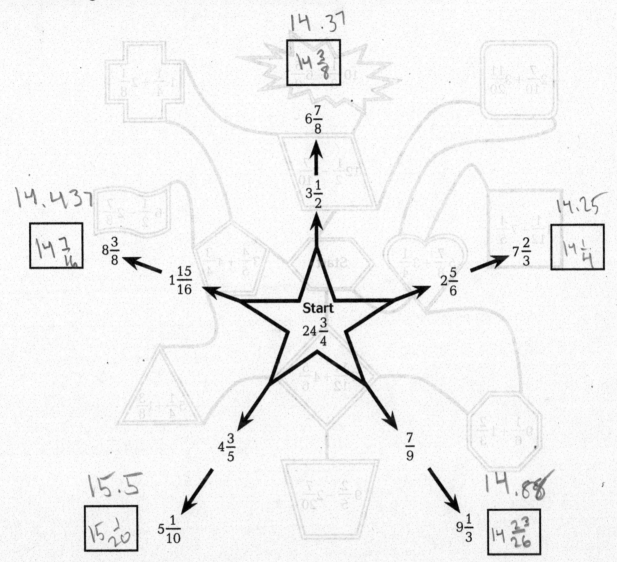

14.37

$14\frac{3}{8}$

$6\frac{7}{8}$

$3\frac{1}{2}$

14.437

$14\frac{7}{16}$

$8\frac{3}{8}$

$1\frac{15}{16}$

14.25

$14\frac{1}{4}$

$7\frac{2}{3}$

$2\frac{5}{6}$

Start
$24\frac{3}{4}$

$4\frac{3}{5}$

$\frac{7}{9}$

15.5

$15\frac{1}{20}$

$5\frac{1}{10}$

14.88

$14\frac{23}{26}$

$9\frac{1}{3}$

1. **Stretch Your Thinking** Order the answers from least to greatest.

14.25; 14.37; 14.437;
14.88; and 15.5

2. **WRITE Math** Explain how you found the answer to problem 1.

I put my fractions
into decimals than
compared them to
least to greatest.

Name _____

The Path of Least Resistance

Always choose the path with the least value. Do not retrace any parts of the path. What shapes are on this path?

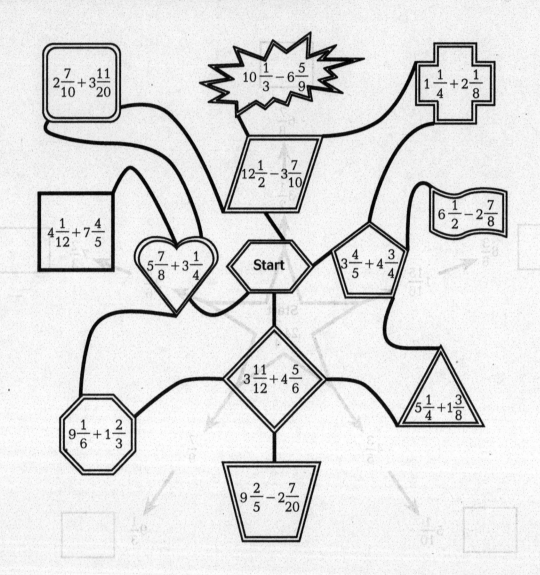

1. Which shape contains the greatest value? What is that value?

   _____

   _____

   _____

2. **Stretch Your Thinking** Use the second lowest value as your first choice. Then use lowest values the rest of the way. What shapes are on the new path?

   _____

   _____

   _____

Matching Fraction Multiplication

Match the model with its corresponding multiplication problem.

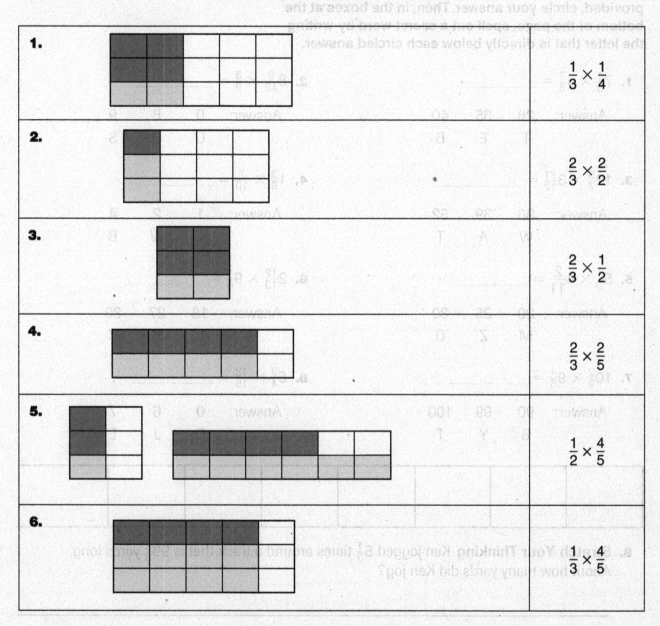

1.	$\frac{1}{3} \times \frac{1}{4}$
2.	$\frac{2}{3} \times \frac{2}{2}$
3.	$\frac{2}{3} \times \frac{1}{2}$
4.	$\frac{2}{3} \times \frac{2}{5}$
5.	$\frac{1}{2} \times \frac{4}{5}$
6.	$\frac{1}{3} \times \frac{4}{5}$

7. **WRITE Math** Explain how you decided which problem correlated with the model in Exercise 3.

_____

_____

Name _____

Estimate the Product

Estimate the product. Out of the three choices provided, circle your answer. Then, in the boxes at the bottom of the page, spell out a secret word by writing the letter that is directly below each circled answer.

1. $7\frac{1}{5} \times 4\frac{7}{8} =$ _____

Answer: 28   35   40
         T   E   B

2. $8\frac{9}{12} \times \frac{8}{9} =$ _____

Answer: 0   8   9
         C   D   S

3. $12\frac{5}{7} \times 3\frac{11}{12} =$ _____

Answer: 36   39   52
         W   A   T

4. $1\frac{3}{8} \times \frac{7}{10} =$ _____

Answer: 1   2   4
         I   W   B

5. $5\frac{1}{3} \times 4\frac{2}{11} =$ _____

Answer: 20   25   30
         M   Z   O

6. $2\frac{12}{13} \times 9\frac{1}{6} =$ _____

Answer: 18   27   30
         L   A   C

7. $10\frac{2}{9} \times 9\frac{4}{5} =$ _____

Answer: 90   99   100
         B   Y   T

8. $6\frac{3}{4} \times \frac{13}{15} =$ _____

Answer: 0   6   7
         D   J   E

9. Stretch Your Thinking Ken jogged $5\frac{1}{3}$ times around a track that is $99\frac{2}{3}$ yards long. About how many yards did Ken jog?

_____

_____

Multiplication Expression Match

Draw a line to match the multiplication expression on the left to the equivalent expression or fraction on the right. Some expressions will have more than one match.

1.		2.	
	$4 \times \frac{1}{4}$		$\frac{1}{4} \times \frac{1}{4}$
$8 \times \frac{3}{4} =$	$12 \times \frac{1}{2}$	$\frac{1}{2} \times \frac{1}{8} =$	$\frac{1}{16}$
	$4 \times \frac{3}{8}$		$\frac{2}{1} \times \frac{8}{1}$
3.		4.	
	$\frac{2}{27}$		$\frac{3}{10} + \frac{1}{5}$
$\frac{2}{3} \times 9 =$	$18 \times \frac{1}{6}$	$\frac{5}{6} \times \frac{3}{5} =$	$\frac{5}{3} \times \frac{6}{5}$
	2×3		$\frac{4}{8}$
5.		6.	
	$\frac{1}{12} \times 12$		$\frac{5}{9} \times \frac{6}{8}$
$12 \times \frac{1}{12} =$	$\frac{12}{12}$	$\frac{4}{9} \times \frac{7}{8} =$	$\frac{8}{18} \times \frac{21}{24}$
	$8 \times \frac{1}{8}$		$\frac{14}{32}$

7. **Stretch Your Thinking** Write two multiplication expressions with fractions that are equivalent to the expression: $\frac{3}{4} \times \frac{2}{3}$.

_____

_____

8. WRITE Math ▸ If you reverse the order of the two fractions in a multiplication sentence, will the answer remain the same? Explain your answer.

_____

_____

_____

_____

_____

Mixed Numbers with Missing Numbers

Use the numbers below the multiplication sentence to make the sentence true. Write the numbers in the boxes.

1. $3\dfrac{2}{\boxed{}} \times \dfrac{\boxed{}}{3} = 2\dfrac{4}{15}$

   Answer choices: 2 5

2. $1\dfrac{7}{8} \times \dfrac{1}{4} = \dfrac{\boxed{}}{\boxed{}}$

   Answer choices: 7 15 24 32

3. $2\dfrac{\boxed{}}{6} \times \dfrac{\boxed{}}{4} = 2\dfrac{1}{8}$

   Answer choices: 2 3 5

4. $4\dfrac{1}{\boxed{}} \times 3\dfrac{3}{7} = 15\dfrac{3}{\boxed{}}$

   Answer choices: 2 3 7

5. $\boxed{}\dfrac{1}{3} \times \boxed{}\dfrac{9}{10} = 10\dfrac{2}{15}$

   Answer choices: 1 5 6

6. $2\dfrac{3}{8} \times \boxed{}\dfrac{1}{\boxed{}} = 15\dfrac{7}{16}$

   Answer choices: 1 2 4 6

7. $\boxed{}\dfrac{4}{5} \times \boxed{}\dfrac{1}{4} = \boxed{}\dfrac{17}{20}$

   Answer choices: 1 3 5

8. $2\dfrac{4}{\boxed{}} \times 4\dfrac{\boxed{}}{6} = 12\dfrac{\boxed{}}{7}$

   Answer choices: 3 5 7

9. $\boxed{}\dfrac{2}{3} \times \dfrac{\boxed{}}{4} = 1\dfrac{1}{\boxed{}}$

   Answer choices: 1 4 6

10. $\dfrac{3}{\boxed{}} \times \boxed{}\dfrac{1}{8} = 1\dfrac{7}{8}$

    Answer choices: 3 5 6

11. What is the missing number for the following sentence?

    $8\dfrac{1}{\boxed{}} \times 1\dfrac{1}{3} = 11\dfrac{1}{3}$

12. **WRITE Math** Describe a method you used to solve the problems above.

    _____

    _____

    _____

Name _____

Fraction Division Grids

Below the grid in the problem is a division expression. Draw a
fraction strip model to show the quotient. Then, in the grid, find
three squares in a row, column, or diagonal that have the same
quotient. Circle that row, column, or diagonal.

1.

$10 \div \frac{1}{2}$	$\frac{1}{5} \div 2$	$3 \div \frac{3}{8}$
$\frac{3}{4} \div \frac{1}{8}$	$1 \div \frac{1}{8}$	$2 \div \frac{1}{8}$
$4 \div \frac{1}{2}$	$2 \div \frac{1}{2}$	$\frac{3}{4} \div \frac{3}{8}$

$2 \div \frac{1}{4}$

2.

$\frac{1}{2} \div 9$	$12 \div 2$	$2 \div 6$
$3 \div \frac{1}{6}$	$3 \div \frac{1}{2}$	$4 \div 3$
$\frac{3}{4} \div 9$	$\frac{1}{3} \div 4$	$\frac{1}{4} \div 3$

$\frac{1}{2} \div 6$

3.

$1 \div \frac{1}{5}$	$\frac{4}{5} \div \frac{2}{5}$	$\frac{1}{2} \div \frac{1}{8}$
$\frac{8}{5} \div \frac{4}{5}$	$\frac{1}{2} \div \frac{1}{2}$	$3 \div \frac{3}{4}$
$\frac{1}{4} \div 2$	$\frac{8}{5} \div \frac{1}{10}$	$\frac{1}{3} \div \frac{1}{12}$

$\frac{4}{5} \div \frac{1}{5}$

4.

$1 \div \frac{1}{4}$	$\frac{5}{6} \div \frac{5}{12}$	$2 \div \frac{1}{3}$
$2 \div \frac{1}{4}$	$\frac{1}{4} \div \frac{1}{8}$	$1 \div \frac{1}{3}$
$4 \div 8$	$\frac{1}{2} \div \frac{1}{4}$	$\frac{3}{4} \div 2$

$\frac{3}{4} \div \frac{3}{8}$

5. Stretch Your Thinking Find the quotient $\frac{1}{4} \div 2\frac{1}{2}$. Draw a model. Explain how your model
represents the quotient.

_____

_____

_____

E27

Hidden Numbers

**Sarah estimated the quotient of each problem. What numbers
could be hiding in the problems? Fill in the blanks.**
Hint: There is more than one correct answer for each problem.

1. $5\frac{5}{6} \div$ _____

Estimated quotient: 3

2. $15\frac{5}{7} \div$ _____

Estimated quotient: 2

3. _____ $\div \frac{3}{7}$

Estimated quotient: 6

4. _____ $\div 5\frac{8}{10}$

Estimated quotient: 3

5. $19\frac{9}{11} \div$ _____

Estimated quotient: 5

6. $9\frac{2}{9} \div$ _____

Estimated quotient: 1

7. _____ $\div 1\frac{6}{7}$

Estimated quotient: 11

8. _____ $\div 3\frac{8}{10}$

Estimated quotient: 4

9. **WRITE Math** ▸ Why is it helpful to know how to estimate quotients?

_____

_____

_____

Name _____

Funny Fractions

**Find the quotient. Write the answer in simplest form.
Then match the letters from the boxes to the quotients
below to answer the riddle.**

$\frac{3}{4} \div \frac{2}{3}$ E	$5 \div \frac{1}{4}$ C	$\frac{1}{10} \div \frac{5}{7}$ T
$\frac{7}{8} \div \frac{1}{4}$ Y	$\frac{4}{5} \div \frac{1}{3}$ I	$\frac{9}{10} \div \frac{3}{4}$ H
$\frac{3}{5} \div \frac{7}{10}$ N	$\frac{1}{6} \div \frac{5}{8}$ E	$8 \div \frac{2}{3}$ S
$\frac{1}{5} \div \frac{5}{6}$ D	$\frac{4}{9} \div \frac{2}{3}$ H	$\frac{1}{4} \div \frac{5}{8}$ A

Riddle:

What did the fraction say to its reciprocal during gymnastics class?

$$\overline{\frac{2}{3}} \quad \overline{1\frac{1}{8}} \quad \overline{3\frac{1}{2}} \, , \quad \overline{\frac{6}{7}} \quad \overline{2\frac{2}{5}} \quad \overline{20} \quad \overline{\frac{4}{15}}$$

$$\overline{1\frac{1}{5}} \quad \overline{\frac{4}{15}} \quad \overline{\frac{2}{5}} \quad \overline{\frac{6}{25}} \quad \overline{12} \quad \overline{\frac{7}{50}} \quad \overline{\frac{2}{5}} \quad \overline{\frac{6}{7}} \quad \overline{\frac{6}{25}} \, !$$

_____

_____

Mixed Number Division Balloons

Insert the letter in the balloon above the reciprocal on the right into the balloon above the divisor on the left. In the balloon above the dividend, write the number of the correct quotient from the list on the bottom.

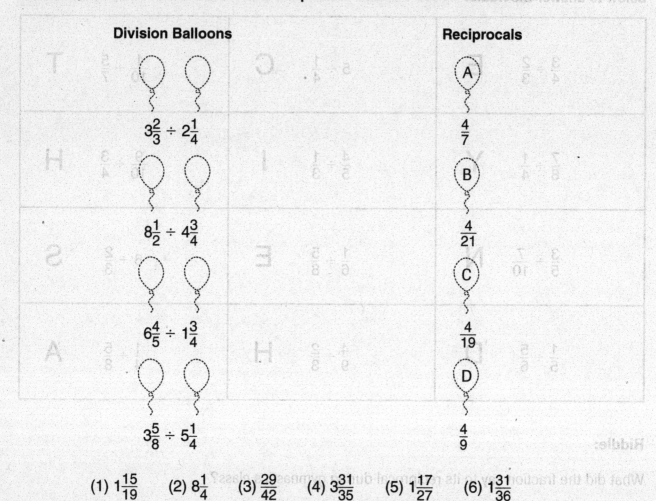

Division Balloons

$3\frac{2}{3} \div 2\frac{1}{4}$

$8\frac{1}{2} \div 4\frac{3}{4}$

$6\frac{4}{5} \div 1\frac{3}{4}$

$3\frac{5}{8} \div 5\frac{1}{4}$

Reciprocals

A

$\frac{4}{7}$

B

$\frac{4}{21}$

C

$\frac{4}{19}$

D

$\frac{4}{9}$

(1) $1\frac{15}{19}$ (2) $8\frac{1}{4}$ (3) $\frac{29}{42}$ (4) $3\frac{31}{35}$ (5) $1\frac{17}{27}$ (6) $1\frac{31}{36}$

1. Write $6\frac{11}{12} \div 7\frac{6}{11}$ as a multiplication expression using fractions greater than 1. How can you simplify the expression?

_____

2. [WRITE Math] Write the steps for dividing two mixed numbers.

_____

_____

_____

Now Arriving, Flight 5⅔ ...

The table below shows flight times and distances from San Francisco
International Airport to other airports. Answer the questions that
follow. Write your answers as fractions in simplest form.

San Francisco International Airport			
Destination	**Departure (Leaves)**	**Arrival (San Francisco Time)**	**Distance**
San Diego, CA	8:30 A.M.	12:00 P.M.	525 mi
Portland, OR	9:45 A.M.	12:00 P.M.	638 mi
Santa Fe, NM	10:00 A.M.	3:20 P.M.	1,200 mi
San Antonio, TX	10:10 A.M.	5:20 P.M.	1,793 mi
Atlanta, GA	2:15 P.M.	10:00 P.M.	2,465 mi

1. What is the travel time for a flight from San Francisco to Santa Fe?

_____

2. How many hours longer is a flight to San Antonio than a flight to Portland?

_____

3. How many times longer (by hours) is a flight to Atlanta than a flight to San Diego?

_____

4. How many hours longer is a flight to San Diego than a flight to Portland?

_____

5. How many times longer (by hours) is a flight to Atlanta than a flight to Santa Fe?

_____

6. The airline has six flights per day to Portland. How many total hours does the airline fly to Portland?

_____

7. An airline determines its rates by charging ⅕ of a dollar per mile. How much do flights to San Diego and Atlanta cost?

_____

_____

_____

8. WRITE Math ▷ Explain how to write 2 hours and 20 minutes as a mixed number.

_____

_____

_____

_____

Name _____

Mental Math Fraction Translation

Complete an equivalent expression that you can use for mental math. Then find the answer.

1. $\frac{1}{8} \times \frac{2}{9} =$

$\frac{1}{4} \times \dfrac{\boxed{}}{9} =$ _____

2. $3\frac{1}{3} \times 5\frac{7}{10} =$

$\dfrac{\boxed{}}{1} \times \dfrac{\boxed{}}{1} =$ _____

3. $20 \times 7\frac{1}{2} =$

$\dfrac{\boxed{}}{1} \times \dfrac{\boxed{}}{\boxed{}} =$ _____

4. $\frac{5}{6} \div \frac{2}{3} =$

$\dfrac{\boxed{}}{2} \times \dfrac{\boxed{}}{2} =$ _____

5. $21 \div \frac{7}{15} =$

$\dfrac{\boxed{}}{1} \times \dfrac{\boxed{}}{\boxed{}} =$ _____

6. $35 \div 3\frac{3}{4} =$

$\dfrac{7}{\boxed{}} \times \dfrac{\boxed{}}{\boxed{}} =$ _____

7. $1\frac{5}{8} \div \frac{3}{10} =$

$\dfrac{\boxed{}}{\boxed{}} \times \dfrac{5}{\boxed{}} =$ _____

8. $4\frac{4}{5} \div 3\frac{3}{7} =$

$\dfrac{\boxed{}}{1} \times \dfrac{\boxed{}}{\boxed{}} =$ _____

9. $2\frac{1}{6} \div 5\frac{1}{4} =$

$\dfrac{\boxed{}}{\boxed{}} \times \dfrac{\boxed{}}{\boxed{}} =$ _____

10. $2\frac{1}{7} \div \frac{5}{6} =$

$\dfrac{\boxed{}}{5} \times \dfrac{\boxed{}}{5} =$ _____

11. $3\frac{3}{5} \div \frac{3}{8} =$

$\dfrac{\boxed{}}{5} \times \dfrac{\boxed{}}{\boxed{}} =$ _____

12. $4\frac{2}{9} \div 3\frac{4}{5} =$

$\dfrac{\boxed{}}{\boxed{}} \times \dfrac{5}{\boxed{}} =$ _____

13. Simplify the multiplication problem below so that you can use mental math to find the answer. Write the answer.

$\frac{7}{10} \times \frac{2}{9} \times \frac{6}{21} =$

_____

_____

14. 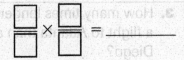 Luz simplified $6\frac{1}{3} \div 2\frac{1}{4}$ to $\frac{19}{1} \times \frac{4}{3}$. Explain the error that Luz made.

_____

_____

_____

_____

Equivalent Fruit

Match each description with an equivalent ratio.

1. bananas to apples	$\frac{2}{10}$
2. apples to fruit	17 to 16
3. strawberries to bananas and oranges	40:10
4. fruit to bananas	10 to 8
5. not oranges to not apples	100:100

6. **WRITE Math** One math class has a greater number of students than the other. However, both classes have a ratio of 5 boys to 6 girls. How is this possible? Give an example.

_____

_____

_____

Matching Rates

Circle all the rates that are equivalent.

1. 340 pages in 20 days 420 pages in 10 days 450 pages in 30 days 210 pages in 5 days	**2.** 200 mi in 10 days 300 mi in 15 days 400 mi in 25 days 500 mi in 30 days
3. 128 jumps in 6 hr 256 jumps in 18 hr 256 jumps in 12 hr 16 jumps in 1 hr	**4.** 320 items in 5 pkg 212 Items in 4 pkg 108 items in 2 pkg 159 items in 3 pkg
5. 120 countries in 3 days 23 countries in 2 days 15 countries in 1 day 46 countries in 4 days	**6.** 60 mi in 2 hr 180 mi in 3 hr 90 mi in 3 hr 120 mi in 4 hr
7. 12 problems in 2 min 15 problems in 3 min 16 problems in 4 min 20 problems in 5 min	**8.** 42 mi on 3 gal 58 mi on 2 gal 51 mi on 3 gal 87 mi on 3 gal
9. 80 apples in 10 sec 48 apples in 6 sec 96 apples in 12 sec 8 apples in 1 sec	**10.** 11 hops in 15 sec 66 hops in 30 sec 88 hops in 120 sec 22 hops in 20 sec
11. 155 ft in 5 hrs 93 ft in 3 hrs 31 ft in 1 hr 62 ft in 4 hrs	**12.** 6 yd in 2 days 15 yd in 3 days 105 yd in 21 days 12 yd in 3 days
13. 105 jacks in 3 bags 210 jacks in 6 bags 240 jacks in 8 bags 35 jacks in 1 bag	**14.** 768 revolutions in 12 min 832 revolutions in 14 min 448 revolutions in 7 min 1,664 revolutions in 26 min

The Path of Ratios

Draw a line to connect each ratio to the correct model.

$\frac{18}{24}$	
$\frac{12}{20}$	
$\frac{16}{24}$	
$\frac{10}{35}$	
$\frac{42}{54}$	
$\frac{15}{18}$	

Name _____

Sunshine Proportions

Circle the value of x that makes a proportion.

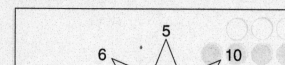

$$\frac{5}{6} = \frac{x}{30}$$

5, 10, 6, 15, 12, 20, 18, 25

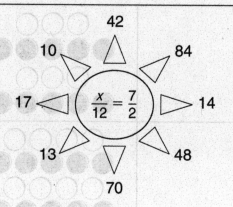

$$\frac{x}{12} = \frac{7}{2}$$

42, 84, 10, 14, 17, 48, 13, 70

$$\frac{60}{24} = \frac{15}{x}$$

75, 6, 45, 8, 39, 30, 69, 21

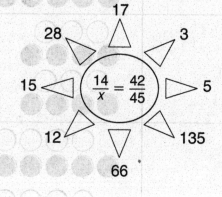

$$\frac{14}{x} = \frac{42}{45}$$

17, 3, 28, 5, 15, 135, 12, 66

$$\frac{x}{2} = \frac{125}{10}$$

2,500, 45, 135, 35, 5, 25, 250, 117

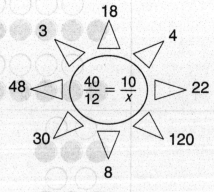

$$\frac{40}{12} = \frac{10}{x}$$

18, 4, 3, 22, 48, 120, 30, 8

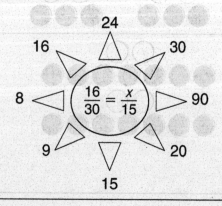

$$\frac{16}{30} = \frac{x}{15}$$

24, 30, 16, 90, 8, 20, 9, 15

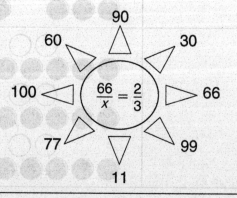

$$\frac{66}{x} = \frac{2}{3}$$

90, 30, 60, 66, 100, 99, 77, 11

Where Are The Words?

Write a word problem to go along with each proportion.
Then solve the proportion.

1. _____ _____ _____ _____	$\dfrac{d}{72} = \dfrac{200}{25}$ $d = \$\underline{\hspace{2cm}}$
2. _____ _____ _____ _____	$\dfrac{8}{160} = \dfrac{h}{60}$ $c = \underline{\hspace{2cm}}$ days
3. _____ _____ _____ _____	$\dfrac{10}{15} = \dfrac{18}{n}$ $n = \underline{\hspace{2cm}}$ games

Percent Pictures

Follow the code to find the hidden picture.

0.9	$\frac{3}{5}$	$\frac{1}{4}$	0.06	$\frac{9}{10}$	0.66	0.32
1.50	5	0.5	$\frac{16}{32}$	$\frac{1}{2}$	0.77	4.5
0.04	$\frac{65}{77}$	$\frac{11}{22}$	$\frac{9}{20}$	$\frac{3}{6}$	0.06	$\frac{44}{100}$
$\frac{16}{31}$	$\frac{11}{100}$	0.500	$\frac{50}{100}$	0.50	0.14	$\frac{1}{5}$
$\frac{50}{120}$	0.12	$\frac{12}{25}$	0.4	$\frac{40}{60}$	0.004	0.88
$\frac{1}{1}$	0.400	1	$\frac{4}{10}$	0.03	$\frac{6}{15}$	$\frac{5}{6}$
0.07	6.5	$\frac{8}{20}$	$\frac{2}{5}$	$\frac{40}{100}$	0.99	0.43
0.29	0.045	$\frac{17}{20}$	0.40	0.730	0.83	$\frac{87}{100}$
$\frac{1}{7}$	0.15	$\frac{6}{23}$	0.58	$\frac{46}{100}$	0.91	1.11

1. Color numbers equivalent to 50% red.

2. Color numbers equivalent to 45% yellow.

3. Color numbers equivalent to 40% green.

What is the hidden picture?

_____

Fraction, Decimal, Percent Soup

Use the fractions, decimals, percents, and ratios in the soup bowl
below to write the equivalent answers for each square. You will not
use all of the values in the bowl.

RATIO	FRACTION	RATIO	FRACTION	RATIO	FRACTION
4 out of 5	_____	_____	$\frac{3}{8}$	_____	_____
				0.74	
DECIMAL	**PERCENT**	**DECIMAL**	**PERCENT**	**DECIMAL**	**PERCENT**
RATIO	**FRACTION**	**RATIO**	**FRACTION**	**RATIO**	**FRACTION**
26 out of 40	_____	_____	_____	0.33 out of 100	_____
			142%		
DECIMAL	**PERCENT**	**DECIMAL**	**PERCENT**	**DECIMAL**	**PERCENT**

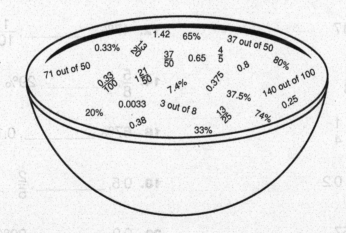

1.42 65%
0.33% $\frac{2}{3}$ 37 out of 50
71 out of 50 $\frac{37}{50}$ 0.65 $\frac{4}{5}$ 80%
$\frac{0.33}{100}$ $\frac{21}{50}$ 0.8
7.4% 0.375 37.5% 140 out of 100
20% 0.0033 3 out of 8 0.25
0.38 $\frac{13}{25}$ 74%
33%

1. **Stretch Your Thinking** Write the
   numbers and ratios that you did not
   use in order from least to greatest.

2. **WRITE Math** Explain how to change
   86% into an equivalent ratio written in
   simplest form.

_____

_____

_____

_____

_____

_____

_____

_____

Name _____

Numbers in the Middle

For 1–10, complete the set of numbers written in order from least to greatest. Each set should contain a fraction, a decimal, and a percent.

1. 10%, $\dfrac{3}{8}$ _____ , 0.58

2. 1%, _____ , $\dfrac{1}{2}$

3. $\dfrac{1}{10}$, _____ , 0.24

4. 0.2, _____ , $\dfrac{4}{5}$

5. $\dfrac{1}{8}$, _____ , 73%

6. 13%, _____ , 0.87

7. $\dfrac{1}{100}$, _____ , 87%

8. 0.19, _____ , 43%

9. 0.34, _____ , 81%

10. $\dfrac{1}{4}$, _____ , 0.9

For 11–20, complete the set of numbers written in order from greatest to least. Each set should contain a fraction, a decimal, and a percent.

11. $\dfrac{5}{6}$, _____ , 0.17

12. 47%, _____ , $\dfrac{1}{10}$

13. 0.8, _____ , $\dfrac{1}{8}$

14. $\dfrac{5}{8}$, _____ , 29%

15. 79%, _____ , $\dfrac{1}{4}$

16. 67%, _____ , 0.15

17. 53%, _____ , 0.2

18. 0.5, _____ , $\dfrac{2}{5}$

19. $\dfrac{4}{5}$, _____ , 0.57

20. 0.9, _____ , 20%

21. **WRITE Math** ▸ Explain the approach you used to solve the problems above.

_____

_____

_____

_____

Name _____

Percent Wheels

Choose from the numbers below to complete the percent wheels.
The first one in Wheel 1 has been done for you.

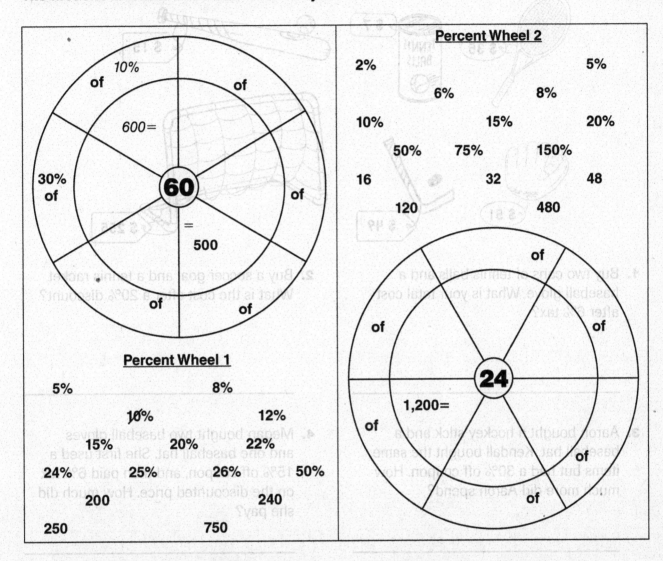

Percent Wheel 1

5%	8%
10%	12%
15%	20%	22%
24%	25%	26%	50%
200	240
250	750

Percent Wheel 2

2%		5%
6%	8%	
10%	15%	20%
50%	75%	150%
16	32	48
120	480	

1. **Stretch Your Thinking** Write a percent problem where the answer is 80.

_____

_____

_____

2. **WRITE Math** Is 150% of 25 equal to 25% of 150? Explain your answer.

_____

_____

_____

_____

Name _____

Time to Shop!

Use the items in the sports store to solve the problems.

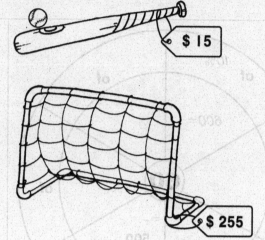

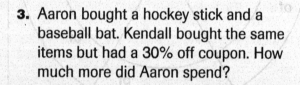

1. Buy two cans of tennis balls and a baseball glove. What is your total cost after 6% tax?

_____

2. Buy a soccer goal and a tennis racket. What is the cost after a 20% discount?

_____

3. Aaron bought a hockey stick and a baseball bat. Kendall bought the same items but had a 30% off coupon. How much more did Aaron spend?

_____

4. Megan bought two baseball gloves and one baseball bat. She first used a 15% off coupon, and then paid 6% tax on the discounted price. How much did she pay?

_____

5. **WRITE Math** ▶ Explain why tax and discounts are based on percentages, rather than flat rates.

_____

_____

_____

_____

Way to Go!

The Gonzalez family went on a vacation to the beach, an amusement park, a national monument, and a state park. They drove to a new place each day, spent the day, and left the following morning. They arrived at 11:47 A.M., 11:33 A.M., 10:21 A.M., 12:31 P.M., and 11:01 A.M., but not in the order shown. The driving time between places and the departure times are shown on the map. List each place they visited in order, along with the time they arrived. Start and end at Home.

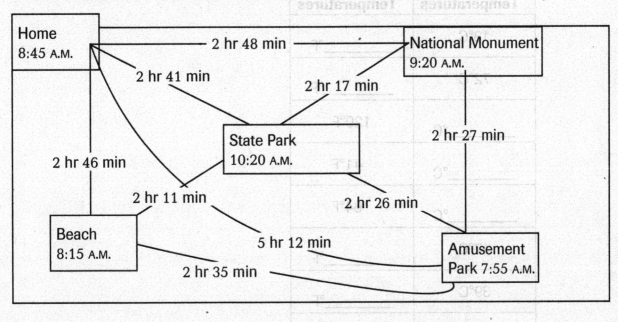

_____

_____

_____

1. Stretch Your Thinking Create new arrival times and different paths to the four places. Starting from Home, list each place they visited in order, along with the time they arrived.

_____

_____

_____

_____

2. WRITE Math Explain how you found the solution to the problem above.

_____

_____

_____

_____

Missing Temperatures

Alana is completing this table of temperature conversions.
Use the formulas $C = \frac{5}{9}(F - 32)$ or $F = \frac{9}{5}C + 32$ to help her.
Round to the nearest tenth of a degree.

Celsius Temperatures	Fahrenheit Temperatures
13°C	_____°F
72°C	_____°F
_____°C	120°F
_____°C	41°F
_____°C	64°F
47°C	_____°F
39°C	_____°F
_____°C	81°F
65°C	_____°F
_____°C	97°F

1. **Stretch Your Thinking** Alana converted 73°F to degrees Celsius and got 87°C. Without calculating, explain how you immediately know that her answer is incorrect. Look at each pair of values in your completed table to identify a relationship.

_____

_____

_____

_____

Lotta Giga Nano

The metric system has linear units that are larger than a kilometer.
The metric system also has linear units that are smaller than a millimeter.
Some of them are given in the table below.

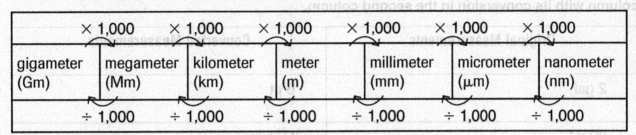

To convert from one unit to the next, multiply or divide by 1,000.

Write *multiply* or *divide*. Decide how many times you multiply or divide
by 1,000 to solve for the variable. Then find the value of the variable.

1. 24 Mm = a m

_____

_____

2. 458 μm = c m

_____

_____

3. 5 km = c m

_____

_____

4. 8 nm = b m

_____

_____

5. 971 Gm = a m

_____

_____

6. 12 nm = d mm

_____

_____

7. 38 mm = a km

_____

_____

8. 7 Gm = b Mm

_____

_____

9. 795 nm = d Mm

_____

_____

10. 156 km = a m

_____

_____

Mixed Up Capacity

The measurements in the first column were converted to other
units with the results in the second column. However, the rows
got mixed up. Connect each measurement in the first
column with its conversion in the second column.

Original Measurements	Converted Measurements
2 gal	6 pt
89 mL	56 cups
8 pt	8 qt
3 qt	35 gal
8.9 L	500 daL
28 pints	500 dL
89 hL	0.0089 kL
113 cups	904 fl oz
140 qt	8.9 kL
5 kL	0.89 dL
0.5 hL	1 gal

1. **WRITE Math** Explain how you could convert 152 cups
to gallons.

_____

_____

_____

Mixed Up Weight and Mass

The measurements in the first column were converted to other units with the results in the second column. However, the rows got mixed up. Connect each measurement in the first column with its conversion in the second column.

Original Measurements	Converted Measurements
4.6 hg	2.6 lb
0.56 lb	8.884 hg
41.6 oz	1.5 T
3,000 lb	4,600 dg
4.6 g	4,500 lb
128 oz	0.884 dag
88.4 dg	8.96 oz
2.25 T	4,600 mg
600,000 dag	6,000 lb
88,840 cg	6,000 kg
3 T	8 lb

1. **WRITE Math** Explain how you could convert $\frac{3}{4}$ tons to ounces.

_____

_____

_____

The Path Less Traveled

Find a 40-cm path from Start to End. Write the letters of the path, from Start to End. Measure line segments to the nearest cm.

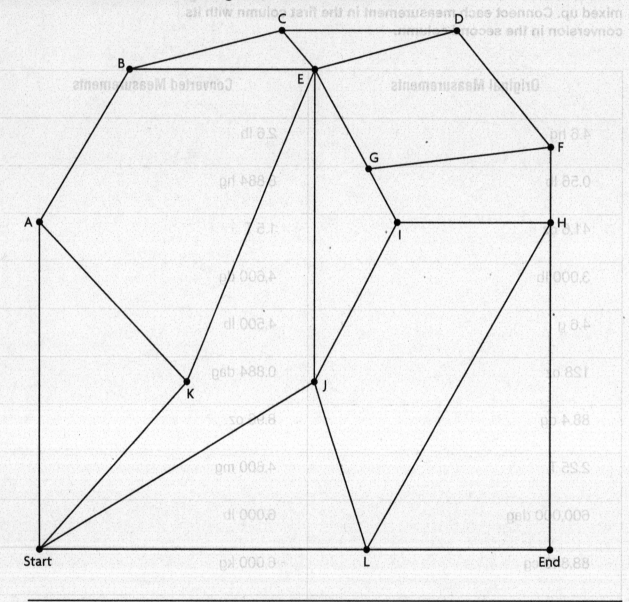

1. **Stretch Your Thinking** Find a different 40-cm path.

_____

2. [WRITE Math] Explain how you found the answer to Problem 1.

_____

_____

On Your Mark, Get Set, GO!!!!!

The car that travels farther, wins. Name the car that wins each race.

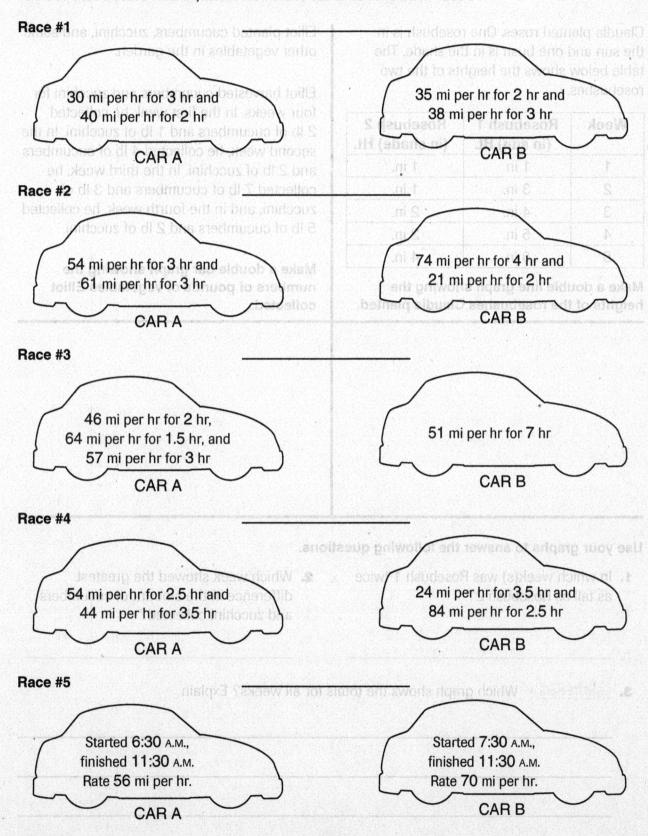

Race #1 _____

30 mi per hr for 3 hr and
40 mi per hr for 2 hr

CAR A

35 mi per hr for 2 hr and
38 mi per hr for 3 hr

CAR B

Race #2 _____

54 mi per hr for 3 hr and
61 mi per hr for 3 hr

CAR A

74 mi per hr for 4 hr and
21 mi per hr for 2 hr

CAR B

Race #3 _____

46 mi per hr for 2 hr,
64 mi per hr for 1.5 hr, and
57 mi per hr for 3 hr

CAR A

51 mi per hr for 7 hr

CAR B

Race #4 _____

54 mi per hr for 2.5 hr and
44 mi per hr for 3.5 hr

CAR A

24 mi per hr for 3.5 hr and
84 mi per hr for 2.5 hr

CAR B

Race #5 _____

Started 6:30 A.M.,
finished 11:30 A.M.
Rate 56 mi per hr.

CAR A

Started 7:30 A.M.,
finished 11:30 A.M.
Rate 70 mi per hr.

CAR B

Gardening Graphs

Claudia and Elliot have a garden. Use the information to make graphs that represent the data.

Claudia planted roses. One rosebush is in the sun and one bush is in the shade. The table below shows the heights of the two rosebushes.

Week	Rosebush 1 (in sun) Ht.	Rosebush 2 (in shade) Ht.
1	1 in.	1 in.
2	3 in.	1 in.
3	4 in.	2 in.
4	5 in.	2 in.
5	8 in.	4 in.

Make a double line graph showing the heights of the rosebushes Claudia planted.

Elliot planted cucumbers, zucchini, and some other vegetables in the garden.

Elliot harvested cucumbers and zucchini for four weeks. In the first week he collected 2 lb of cucumbers and 1 lb of zucchini. In the second week, he collected 4 lb of cucumbers and 2 lb of zucchini. In the third week, he collected 7 lb of cucumbers and 3 lb of zucchini, and in the fourth week, he collected 5 lb of cucumbers and 2 lb of zucchini.

Make a double bar graph showing the numbers of pounds of vegetables Elliot collected.

Use your graphs to answer the following questions.

1. In which week(s) was Rosebush 1 twice as tall as Rosebush 2?

_____

2. Which week showed the greatest difference in the amount of cucumbers and zucchini collected?

_____

3. ⟩WRITE Math⟩ Which graph shows the totals for all weeks? Explain.

_____

_____

Make Circle Graphs

The tables below show data on the magazines students read. Use the tables to make graphs.

Students' Favorite Types of Magazines	
Type of Magazine	Number of Students
Music	38
Sports	76
TV/Movies	24
Clothing/Fashion	62

Pages in Student Entertainment Magazine	
Type of Page	Number of Pages
Articles	30
Photographs	23
Advertisements	45
Public Service	2

1. What percentage of students like music magazines the most?

2. What percentage like sports magazines the most?

3. What percentage like TV and movie magazines the most?

4. What percentage like clothing and fashion magazines the most?

5. Use your percentages Problems 1–4 to make a circle graph of Students' Favorite Magazines.

6. Use the space below to make a circle graph of the types of pages in the student entertainment magazine.

Name _____

Numbers In and Out of This World

Use the tables to find the mean, median, and mode.

1. What is the mean height of the buildings?

_____

2. What is the mode? What is the range?

_____

3. What is the median height of the buildings?

_____

Tallest Buildings by Country	
Country	**Height of Tallest Building**
Spain	820 ft
Nigeria	272 ft
Morocco	377 ft
Austria	663 ft
Bolivia	351 ft
Finland	282 ft
Peru	351 ft
South Africa	732 ft

4. What is the mean number of moons?

_____

5. What is the mode? What is the range?

_____

6. What is the median number of moons?

_____

Number of Known Planetary Moons	
Planet	**Number of Moons**
Mercury	0
Venus	0
Earth	1
Mars	2
Jupiter	63
Saturn	34
Uranus	27
Neptune	13

7. Stretch Your Thinking Scientists argue that Pluto is not a planet. If Pluto is a planet, the median number of moons would change to 3. How many moons is Pluto argued to have?

_____

_____

8. ⟨WRITE Math⟩ ▸ Did you get a decimal answer for any of questions 4–6? Explain how an answer can be a decimal. (There's no such thing as 0.5 moons.)

_____

_____

Serving Up Line Plots and Frequency Tables

Use the space to the right to make a line plot and relative frequency table of the data.

1. The table below shows the number of tables Marisa served at a restaurant.

Number of Tables Served Daily				
8	9	13	12	9
11	8	4	8	11
8	12	7	10	9
9	10	12	8	13
13	7	11	9	10

Make a line plot of the data.

2. What is the mode(s) of the data?

_____

3. What number of tables did Marisa serve least often?

_____

4. The tally chart shows the number of days Marisa worked different hours.

Daily Hours Marisa Worked	
Whole Number of Hours Worked	Tally
0–2 h	ll
3–4 h	ll
5–6 h	ՀՀՀ lll
7–8 h	ՀՀՀ ՀՀՀ l

Make a relative frequency table of the data.

5. Stretch Your Thinking How many days did Marisa work 6 hours or less?

6. How many days did Marisa work 4 hours or less?

_____   _____

7. WRITE Math ▶ How do the line plot and the frequency table help show information about data? Explain.

_____

Plotting Along the Beach

Lifeguards at Stony Beach were told to record data on visitors to the beach one morning. They made the following tables below based on their results.

Ages of Swimmers

12	45	11	65	31	8
38	17	59	5	21	16
68	52	12	3	24	15
16	35	5	9	67	23
25	7	13	19	21	5

Money in Dollars Spent per Family at Refreshment and Souvenir Stands

13	6	25	18	10	29
5	14	15	23	34	9
16	52	26	12	7	38
13	25	31	20	5	6
34	8	11	29	22	30

Make a histogram for the ages of swimmers at the beach for that morning.

Make a stem-and-leaf plot for the number of dollars spent per family at the beach.

1. **Stretch Your Thinking** How many more swimmers at the beach were 10–19 years old than were 40–49 years old?

2. How many families spent $10–$19 at the beach?

3. [WRITE Math] Explain how a histogram and stem-and-leaf plot are similar and how they are different.

_____

_____

© Houghton Mifflin Harcourt Publishing Company

Graphing for a Business

Don and Bryan have a refreshment stand. They want to make graphs of data from their stand for a business plan. Use the information below to determine if the graph is appropriate. If the graph is not appropriate, suggest a type of graph that can be used.

1. Don made two circle graphs. One circle graph shows the amount of money made daily from selling lemonade. The second shows the amount of money made daily from selling water. Is the graph appropriate?

_____

2. Bryan made a line graph based on the following table.

Number of Bottles of Drinks Sold				
	Water	Lemon-ade	Juice	Energy Drink
Bottles Sold	22	13	7	24

Is the graph appropriate?

_____

3. Don made a bar graph based on the following table.

Ages of Customers				
16	28	10	45	17
30	14	24	16	57
63	12	26	33	12
38	42	27	18	60

Is the graph appropriate?

_____

_____

4. Bryan made a double bar graph to show the snacks and drinks sold for five weeks. Is the graph appropriate?

_____

_____

5. Stretch Your Thinking Give a situation involving Don and Bryan's refreshment stand for which a circle graph would be appropriate to display the data.

_____

_____

6. ⬛ WRITE Math ▶ Explain when a double line graph is more appropriate to use than a double bar graph.

_____

_____

_____

Name _____

Match Surveys to Results

The tables below show the results of surveys conducted by a
survey company. Match the tables with the types of surveys
that were used.

Survey: _____

Do You Recycle?		
Sampling Method	Yes	No
Called 1,800 people out of the phone book	985	815

Survey: _____

Do You Recycle?		
Sampling Method	Yes	No
Surveyed 220 people sitting at a park	168	52

Survey: _____

Do You Recycle?		
Sampling Method	Yes	No
Mailed a survey to one college student on the student body list. Then mailed to every 10th student on the list.	72	34

Survey: _____

Do You Recycle?		
Sampling Method	Yes	No
Called all town residents 80 years old and older	61	38

Survey One: A survey of an entire
population of an age group needs to be
performed to find out if a certain age group
is recycling.

Survey Two: A random survey needs to be
performed to find out if residents in a county
are recycling.

Survey Three: A systematic sample needs
to be performed to find out if a certain age
group is recycling.

Survey Four: A convenience survey needs to
be performed to find out if residents in a town
are recycling.

1. **WRITE Math** What are some key words
or situations that helped you determine
which type of surveys were conducted?

_____

_____

_____

2. **Stretch Your Thinking** Make your own
table showing results of a survey and
describe the type of survey the table
represents.

Organize Your Survey

Suppose the information below is responses from a survey you took.
Organize the responses in a line plot and relative frequency table and
answer the questions that follow.

Survey Question: What is your favorite type of
website: sports, entertainment (music, movies, etc.),
games, or websites about animals?

Line plot

Relative Frequency Table

Person	Response
1	Sports
2	Entertainment
3	Entertainment
4	Animals
5	Entertainment
6	Games
7	Sports
8	Games
9	Games
10	Games
11	Games
12	Entertainment
13	Games
14	Animals
15	Entertainment
16	Entertainment
17	Sports
18	Games
19	Games
20	Entertainment
21	Sports
22	Animals
23	Sports
24	Entertainment
25	Games

1. **WRITE Math** What conclusions can you make about the survey results?

_____

_____

_____

How Many Letters in the Bag?

An unknown number of cards are in a bag. Each card has a letter of the alphabet printed on it. A card is randomly drawn and replaced 40 times. Use the results shown below to find the probabilities.

1. What is the experimental probability of selecting each letter? Write your answers as fractions, decimals, and percents.

Letters Picked After 40 Selections

Letter	L	M	N	O	P
Times selected	3	5	15	12	5

L: _____

M: _____

N: _____

O: _____

P: _____

Q: _____

2. You have been asked to take the bag of cards and randomly select and replace a letter 120 times. Use experimental probability to complete the table to the right to predict how many times you will draw each letter.

Letters Picked After 120 Selections

Letter	L	M	N	O	P
Times selected					

3. Stretch Your Thinking Does the chart in Problem 1 give an indication of how many cards are in the bag? Explain.

_____

_____

_____

_____

_____

4. [WRITE Math] You are told that in the bag of cards above, there are 9 cards in all. Write how many cards of each letter you think are in the bag. Explain your predictions.

_____

_____

_____

_____

_____

Probabilities for Different Events

Use the probabilities to color the spinners and marbles, and label the cards with numbers.

1. The probability of spinning green is $\frac{1}{8}$.

The probability of spinning blue is $\frac{1}{4}$.

The probability of spinning yellow is $\frac{1}{4}$.

The probability of not spinning red is $\frac{5}{8}$.

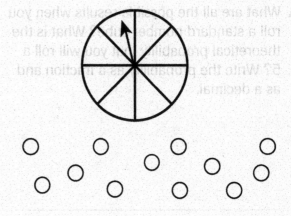

2. The probability of choosing pink is $\frac{1}{3}$.

The probability of choosing black is $\frac{1}{2}$.

The probability of choosing brown is $\frac{1}{6}$.

The probability of choosing purple is 0.

3. The numbers on the cards are any numbers from 1 to 5.

The probability of picking a 3 is 20%.

The probability of picking an even number is 60%.

The probability of picking a 1 is 20%.

The probability of picking a 2 is 40%.

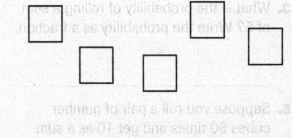

4. Use fractions, decimals, and percents to list all the probabilities when randomly choosing one of the marbles below.

_____

_____

_____

5. 〉WRITE Math 〉 Write a possible event where the probability of choosing or spinning red is $33\frac{1}{3}$%.

_____

_____

_____

_____

_____

Theoretical and Experimental Probability

Use what you know about theoretical and experimental probability to solve these problems.

1. What are all the possible results when you roll a standard number cube? What is the theoretical probability that you will roll a 5? Write the probability as a fraction and as a decimal.

_____

2. Write the missing numbers to show all possible results of rolling *two* number cubes. (**Hint**: Order matters. Think of rolling one cube and then the other. Rolling 1 and then 2 is a different result than rolling 2 and then 1.)

(1, 1) (1, 2) (1, 3) (1, __) (1, __) (1, __)

(2, 1) (2, 2) (2, 3) (__, __) (__, __) (__, __)

(3, 1) (3, 2) (__, __) (__, __) (__, __) (__, __)

(4, 1) (4, 2) (__, __) (__, __) (__, __) (__, __)

(5, 1) (5, 2) (__, __) (__, __) (__, __) (__, __)

(6, 1) (6, 2) (__, __) (__, __) (__, __) (__, __)

3. What is the probability of rolling a sum of 5? Write the probability as a fraction.

_____

4. What sum has the greatest probability? What is that probability?

_____

5. Suppose you roll a pair of number cubes 60 times and get 10 as a sum 4 times. Find the difference between the theoretical and experimental probabilities of getting 10 as a sum.

_____

6. Suppose you roll a pair of number cubes 360 times. What is the most likely number of times you will get a sum of 11? Show your work.

_____

WRITE Math ▷ Justify your method in problem 6.

_____

_____

_____

Name _____

What's In the Jar?

Jars filled with different items are set up at a county fair. The person who comes closest to describing the contents of the jar can keep the jar and its contents as a prize. You are given hints about what is in each jar. Use the hints to predict the contents of each jar.

Jar 1
Filled With 875 Jellybeans

Hint: One at a time 100 people pulled out a jellybean and returned it. The results were 23 green, 18 purple, 34 orange, and 25 black jellybeans.

How many jellybeans of each color are in the jar?

_____

_____

_____

Jar 2
Filled With 1,200 Marbles

Hint: One at a time 150 people pulled out a marble and returned it. The results were 54 red, 33 blue, 18 green, and 45 yellow marbles.

How many marbles of each color are in the jar?

_____

_____

_____

Jar 3
Filled With 2,300 Fake Gems

Hint: One at a time 240 people pulled out a gem and returned it. The results were 85 rubies, 55 pearls, and 100 emeralds.

How many gems of each type are in the jar?

_____

_____

Jar 4
Filled With 650 Coins

Hint: One at a time 75 people pulled out a coin and returned it. The results were 30 pennies, 18 nickels, 15 dimes, 9 quarters, and 3 dollar coins.

How many coins of each type are in the jar?

_____

_____

_____

---

1. **Stretch Your Thinking** Use your answers for Jar 4 to estimate how much money is in the jar.

_____

_____

_____

2. **WRITE Math** How can you check your predictions for the jars?

_____

_____

_____

_____

Draw a Diagram to Find the Combinations

Draw a diagram to solve.

1. Ms. Tiso is putting together softball
   uniforms for the girls' softball team.
   Uniforms must have one cap, one
   shirt/pant suit, and one pair of socks.
   How many different combinations of
   uniforms can she make?

   _____

   _____

   _____

   _____

Cap   **Shirt/Pant Suit**   **Socks**

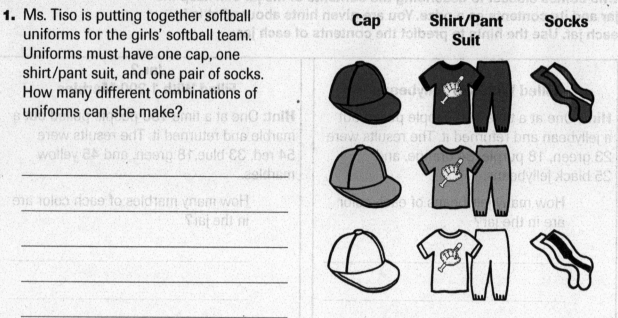

2. Three coins are flipped. How many
   possible outcomes are there? What are
   the outcomes?

   _____

   _____

   _____

3. **Stretch Your Thinking** In Problem 1,
   Ms. Tiso decides to add gray socks as
   a choice for the uniforms. How many
   different combinations does this add?
   What is the total number of combinations
   she can make?

   _____

   _____

4. **WRITE Math** How can drawing a diagram help you solve problems that
   ask for combinations? Explain.

   _____

   _____

   _____

   _____

Which Way Do I Go?

Find a path through the maze so each new integer is greater than
the previous integer. What is the last integer?

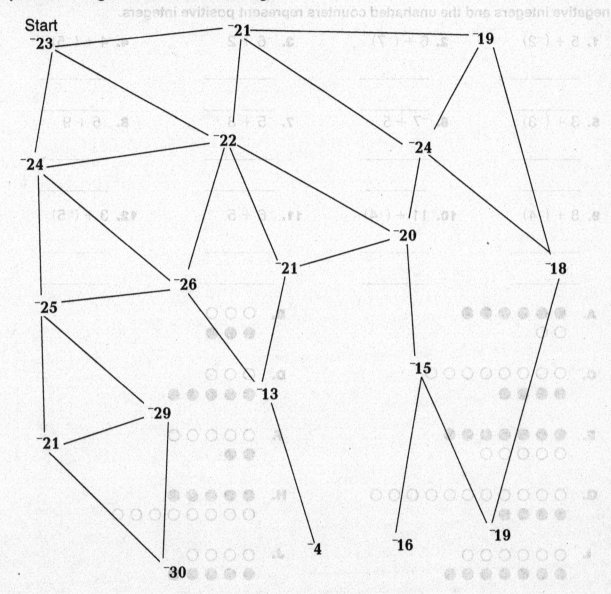

1. **Stretch Your Thinking** Find a path
   through the maze so each new integer is
   less than the previous integer. What is the
   last integer?

2. $\boxed{\text{WRITE Math}}$ How did you find the path
   of decreasing integers?

All Mixed Up

Help Harry match the problems with their models. Write the answer and the letter of the model. The shaded counters represent negative integers and the unshaded counters represent positive integers.

1. $5 + (^-2)$ _____

2. $6 + (^-7)$ _____

3. $^-6 + 2$ _____

4. $4 + (^-5)$ _____

5. $3 + (^-3)$ _____

6. $^-7 + 5$ _____

7. $^-5 + 8$ _____

8. $^-6 + 9$ _____

9. $8 + (^-4)$ _____

10. $11 + (^-4)$ _____

11. $^-6 + 5$ _____

12. $3 + (^-5)$ _____

A. ● ● ● ● ● ●
○ ○

B. ○ ○ ○
● ● ●

C. ○ ○ ○ ○ ○ ○ ○
● ● ● ●

D. ○ ○ ○
● ● ● ● ●

E. ● ● ● ● ● ●
○ ○ ○ ○ ○

F. ○ ○ ○ ○ ○
● ●

G. ○ ○ ○ ○ ○ ○ ○ ○ ○ ○
● ● ● ●

H. ● ● ● ● ●
○ ○ ○ ○ ○ ○ ○

I. ○ ○ ○ ○ ○
● ● ● ● ● ●

J. ○ ○ ○ ○
● ● ● ● ●

K. ● ● ● ● ● ●
○ ○ ○ ○

L. ● ● ● ● ● ●
○ ○ ○ ○ ○ ○ ○

13. Explain how you matched the models and problems.

_____

_____

14. Draw a counter model to represent $^-3 + 5$.

Name _____

What Is the Problem?

Write the expression that each number line models. Then write the sum.

1.

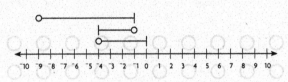

_____

2.

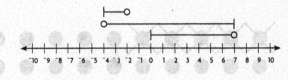

_____

3.

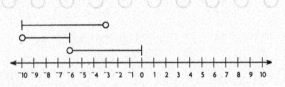

_____

4.

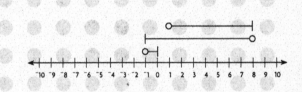

_____

5.

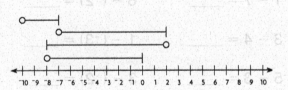

_____

6.

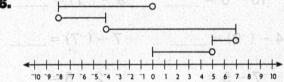

_____

7. Stretch Your Thinking Would you get a different answer if you wrote the integer modeled at the top of the number line first? Explain.

_____

_____

_____

_____

8. Create a number line to model $-5 + 6 + (-4)$.

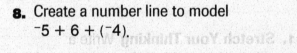
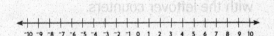

Name _____

Name _____

Name _____

What Is Left?

Brandy marks off shaded counters to show negative answers
and unshaded counters to show positive answers. If she marks
counters for every problem below, how many of each counter
will be left? The first one is done for you.

$^-7 - (^-2) = \underline{\ ^-5\ }$ $6 - (^-4) = \underline{\hspace{1cm}}$ $^-8 - 5 = \underline{\hspace{1cm}}$ $5 - (^-3) = \underline{\hspace{1cm}}$

$^-10 - 6 = \underline{\hspace{1cm}}$ $^-9 - (^-7) = \underline{\hspace{1cm}}$ $^-1 - 7 = \underline{\hspace{1cm}}$ $6 - (^-2) = \underline{\hspace{1cm}}$

$^-4 - (^-9) = \underline{\hspace{1cm}}$ $7 - (^-7) = \underline{\hspace{1cm}}$ $^-3 - 4 = \underline{\hspace{1cm}}$ $1 - (^-3) = \underline{\hspace{1cm}}$

$^-7 - 5 = \underline{\hspace{1cm}}$ $^-2 - 8 = \underline{\hspace{1cm}}$ $^-5 - 3 = \underline{\hspace{1cm}}$ $3 - (^-2) = \underline{\hspace{1cm}}$

Shaded counters left: _____

Unshaded counters left: _____

1. **Stretch Your Thinking** Write a
subtraction problem that can be modeled
with the leftover counters.

_____

_____

2. **Stretch Your Thinking** Change the
subtraction problem from problem 1 into
an addition problem. What is the answer
to the addition problem?

_____

_____

_____

Name _____

Starlight Subtraction

Circle all the subtraction expressions that equal the integer in the center of the star.

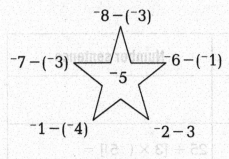

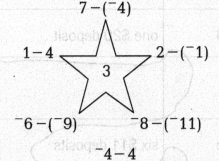

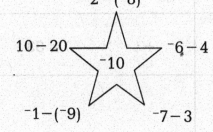

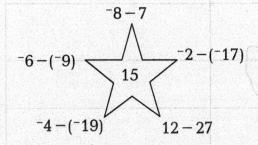

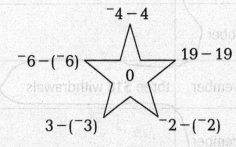

1. Write 4 subtraction expressions that each equal ⁻7.

_____

_____

2. **WRITE Math** What outcome do you get when you subtract a negative integer?

_____

_____

Name _____

Missing Integers

Josiah has a student savings account in which he cannot
have a negative balance for more than one month in a row.
Josiah spilled milk on his ledger. Find the missing information.
Write number sentences to help you.

Date	Deposits/Withdrawals	Balance	Number sentence
January		+25	
February	three $5 withdrawals		$25 + [3 \times (^-5)] =$
April	one $20 deposit		$10 + (1 \times 20) =$
May		$^-18$	$\_\_ + (\_\_ \times \_\_) = \ ^-18$
June	six $11 deposits		$^-18 + (6 \times 11) =$
July		+33	$\_\_ + (\_\_ \times \_\_) = 33$
September		$^-7$	
October		+53	
November	three $18 withdrawals		
December		+43	

1. **WRITE Math** Explain why there is more than one answer possible
   for the "Deposits/Withdrawals" column. Use an example in your answer.

_____

_____

Multiplication Madness

Marcia created a board game with integers. Each player rolls a
die, moves a game piece the number of spaces rolled, and selects
a card. Each card has a multiplication expression whose product
is one of the integers on the board. If the expression on the card
drawn equals the integer on the place where the player landed,
the player wins. Above each integer on the board write a
multiplication expression with at least one negative factor whose
product is that integer.

⁻12	8	⁻4	⁻6	24	⁻15	⁻5	⁻14
⁻72							⁻8
⁻16	Cards						⁻20
6							16
⁻35							30
⁻45			Start				⁻18
⁻1							⁻9
⁻28							10
⁻25							⁻12
36	27	⁻30	⁻7	⁻40	⁻13	4	⁻24

1. **Stretch Your Thinking** If there were
cards for every possible pair of factors,
which integer would have the most
cards?

2. **WRITE Math** Explain how you found the
answer to problem 1.

Name _____

Dazzling Division Ribbons

**The math department made prize ribbons for a math contest.
If the ribbons are handed out in order from least to greatest
quotient, in which order should they be given out?**

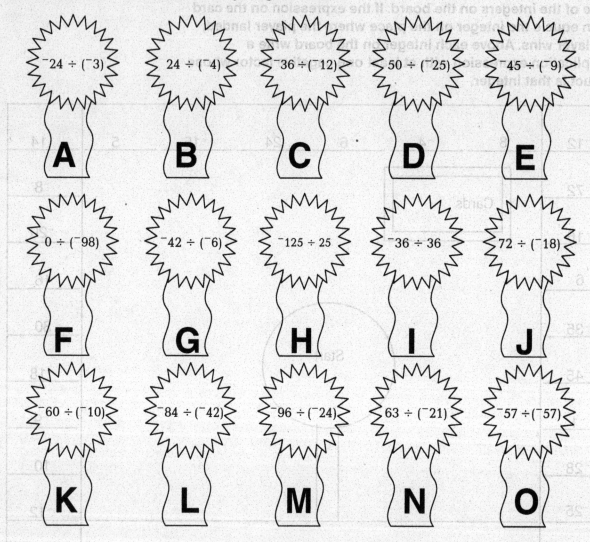

1. What is the sum of all the quotients?

_____

_____

2. WRITE Math ▶ A nonzero number is divided
by itself. What is the quotient? Explain.

_____

_____

Use Diagrams and Other Math Skills

Draw diagrams and use some of your other math skills to solve these problems.

1. A ship's anchor is raised at the rate of 10 meters per minute for 30 seconds. Then it is lowered at the rate of 15 meters per minute for 20 seconds. Then it is raised at the rate of 12 meters per minute for 15 seconds. Its final position is 6 meters below sea level. What was its starting position?

_____

2. A scuba diver descends at the rate of 12 feet per minute for 2 minutes. Then she descends at half that rate for 1 minute. Then she rises at the rate of 8 feet per minute for 2 minutes 30 seconds. Her final position is 22 feet below sea level. What was her starting position?

_____

3. A scuba diver begins at 38 feet below sea level. He rises at the rate of 12 feet per minute for 30 seconds. Then he descends at the same rate for 1 minute 30 seconds. If he then rises at the rate of 10 feet per minute, how long will it take him to reach the surface?

_____

4. There are 8 cones spaced evenly around a circular track. Ed runs at a constant speed around the track. It takes Ed 36 seconds to run from the first cone to the fourth cone. How long does it take Ed to run completely around the track?

_____

5. A marble is chosen randomly from a bag of at least 20 marbles. The only marble colors are red, blue, and yellow. The probability of choosing blue is 2 times the probability of choosing red and half the probability of choosing yellow. The bag has at least how many yellow marbles?

_____

6. A tile is chosen randomly from a bag. The only tile colors are red, blue, and yellow. The probability of choosing red is $\frac{1}{3}$. The probability of choosing blue is half the probability of choosing yellow. The bag has at least how many yellow tiles?

_____

7. **WRITE Math** ▶ Explain how you solved Problem 6.

_____

_____

_____

_____

Ink Blots

Polly's pen leaked ink on an integer or an addition or subtraction sign in each problem. Fill in the missing integer or sign that will make the equation true.

1. $4 + (^-6) \times \square = {}^-14$

2. $[9 + (^-7)] \square\, 5 = 10$

3. $(^-6 - \square) \div 4 = {}^-2$

4. $^-7 - (^-7) \square\, 11 = {}^-11$

5. $\square - 8 \times (^-2) = 4$

6. $[12 \square (^-6)] \div 3 = 6$

7. $5 + (^-6 - \square) = {}^-4$

8. $[\square + (^-9)] \times 2 = {}^-28$

9. $11 \square (^-20) \times 5 = 111$

10. $[^-10 - (^-15)] \square (^-5) = {}^-1$

11. $^-6 \div (^-2) \times \square = {}^-30$

12. $[14 + (^-7)] \times \square = {}^-35$

13. $11 \square 17 \times 7 = {}^-108$

14. $[21 + \square] \div (^-13) = {}^-1$

15. $\square - (^-12) \times 8 = 75$

16. $[15 - \square] \times 9 = 144$

17. $(\square + (^-2)) \times 8 = {}^-80$

18. $[^-18 \square (^-6)] \times (^-4) = 96$

19. $(11 - 12) \times \square = {}^-57$

20. $(24 - \square) \div (^-1) = {}^-16$

21. $[6 - (^-2)] \div \square = 2$

22. $[\square - (^-4)] \times 2 = {}^-12$

23. **Stretch Your Thinking** Rewrite the equation with parentheses or brackets to make the equation true.
$^-6 + (^-12) \div 3 - 7 = {}^-13$

_____

_____

24. **Stretch Your Thinking** Rewrite the equation with parentheses or brackets to make the equation true.
$^-4 - (^-12) + 9 - 8 = {}^-9$

_____

_____

Word Confusion

Write the missing word, number, sign of operation, or variable to make the word sentence match the equation.

1. Three more than a number is _____.

$n +$ _____ $= 12$

2. _____ less than a number is 51.

n _____ $5 = 51$

3. Nine _____ a number is 81.

$9n =$ _____

4. The sum of a number and _____ is 39.8.

_____ $+ 24.8 =$ _____

5. The quotient of a number and _____ is 14.

n _____ $21 =$ _____

6. _____ less than a number is _____.

n _____ $11 = 24$

7. $3\frac{4}{5}$ is _____ more than a number.

_____ $= n + 1\frac{1}{2}$

8. 29.6 less than a _____ is _____.

n _____ $29.6 = 194.8$

9. A number increased by _____ is ⁻24.

$n +$ ⁻11 $=$ _____

10. Fifteen is equal to _____ times a number.

_____ $= 7n$

11. The quotient of a _____ and 11 is 19.3.

$n \div$ _____ $= 19.3$

12. A number _____ by $7\frac{3}{4}$ is _____.

$n -$ _____ $= \frac{1}{2}$

13. The _____ of a number and 3.2 is 174.6.

$n \div$ _____ $=$ _____

14. A number _____ by 11.1 is _____.

$n -$ _____ $=$ ⁻6.3

15. Twice a number is _____.

_____ $n = 54$

16. When a number is _____ by 2.1, the result is 9.9.

$n + 2.1 =$ _____

17. Eleven _____ _____ a number is 913.

$n -$ _____ $=$ _____

18. Twelve minus a _____ is 18.

_____ $- n =$ _____

Stay Balanced!

You learned that an equation must always stay balanced. For each equation, write a number in the box to keep it balanced.

1. $2 + 5 = \boxed{} + 1$

2. $4 + 4 = \boxed{} + 5$

3. $\boxed{} + 4 = 3 + 3$

4. $5 + \boxed{} = 1 + 4$

5. $11 + 4 = \boxed{} + 11$

6. $8 + 7 = 5 + \boxed{}$

7. $2 + \boxed{} = 15 - 9$

8. $5 + 6 = \boxed{} - 1$

9. $\boxed{} - 4 = 8 + 8$

10. $0 + \boxed{} = 14 - 6$

11. 〔WRITE Math〕▶ Explain how you balanced the equations.

_____

_____

_____

Less Is More...and More is Less

Circle the value of the variable that makes the equation true.

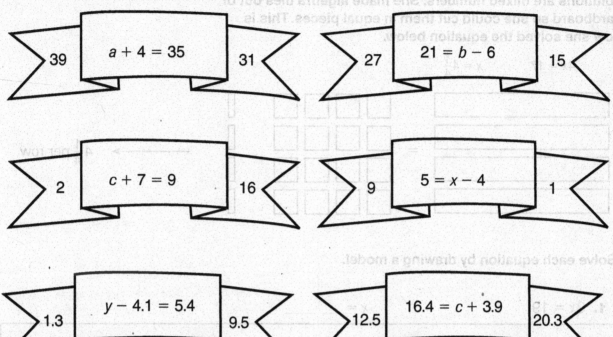

39 $a + 4 = 35$ 31 | 27 $21 = b - 6$ 15

2 $c + 7 = 9$ 16 | 9 $5 = x - 4$ 1

1.3 $y - 4.1 = 5.4$ 9.5 | 12.5 $16.4 = c + 3.9$ 20.3

$10\frac{1}{4}$ $v + 3\frac{3}{4} = 14$ $17\frac{3}{4}$ | $2\frac{5}{6}$ $5\frac{2}{3} = d - 2\frac{5}{6}$ $8\frac{1}{2}$

$1\frac{4}{9}$ $k - 2\frac{5}{9} = 4$ $6\frac{5}{9}$ | $13\frac{3}{4}$ $12\frac{1}{4} = d + 1\frac{1}{2}$ $10\frac{3}{4}$

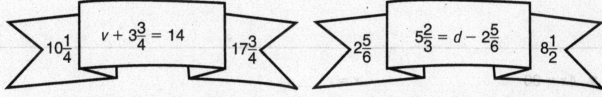

15 $b - 4 = 11$ 7 | 43 $30 = x + 13$ 17

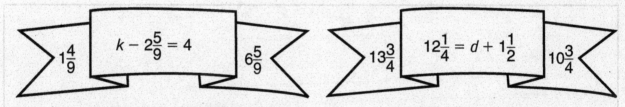

6 $j + 32 = 38$ 70 | 18 $5 = x - 13$ 8

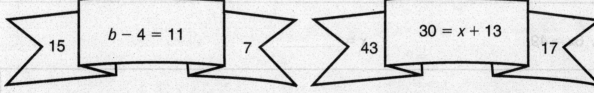

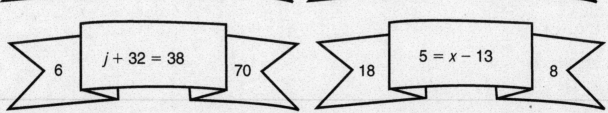

Fractioned Tiles

Sharon wants to use algebra tiles to solve equations whose
solutions are mixed numbers. She made algebra tiles out of
cardboard so she could cut them in equal pieces. This is
how she solved the equation below.

$$4x = 17 \qquad x = 4\frac{1}{4}$$

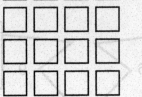 $4\frac{1}{4}$ per row

Solve each equation by drawing a model.

1. $3x = 19$ $\qquad x =$ _____

2. $4x = 30$ $\qquad x =$ _____

3. $6x = 49$ $\qquad x =$ _____

The Path Less Traveled

Solve the equation $\frac{r}{4} = 6$. Then follow the arrow at the solution to
the next equation. Keep doing this until you have solved each
equation. Show the path by giving the solution to each equation.
What letter did you form?

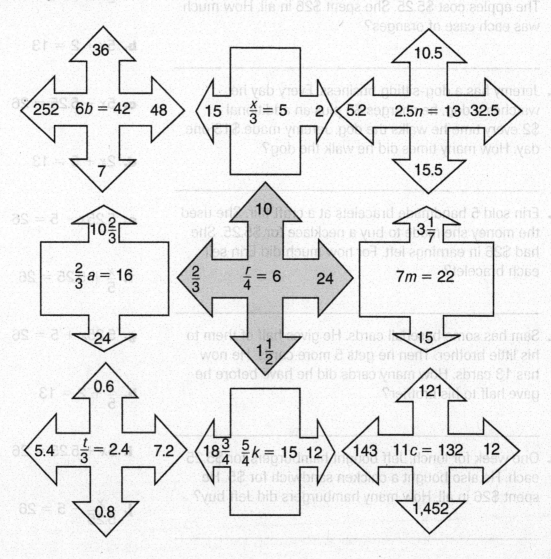

_____

_____

_____

Equation Look-Alikes

**Match the word problem with the equation that can be used to solve it.
Write the letter to show your answer. Then solve the problem.**

1. Julie bought 5 cases of oranges and a bag of apples. The apples cost $5.25. She spent $26 in all. How much was each case of oranges?

_____

a. $\dfrac{x}{2} + 5 = 13$

b. $5x + 2 = 13$

2. Jeremy has a dog-sitting business. Every day he watches a dog, he charges $5 plus an additional $2 every time he walks the dog. Jeremy made $13 one day. How many times did he walk the dog?

_____

c. $5x - 5.25 = 26$

d. $2x + 5 = 13$

3. Erin sold 5 handmade bracelets at a craft fair. She used the money she made to buy a necklace for $5.25. She had $26 in earnings left. For how much did Erin sell each bracelet?

_____

e. $5.25x - 5 = 26$

f. $\dfrac{x}{5} + 5.25 = 26$

4. Sam has some baseball cards. He gives half of them to his little brother. Then he gets 5 more cards. He now has 13 cards. How many cards did he have before he gave half to his brother?

_____

g. $5.25x + 5 = 26$

h. $\dfrac{x}{5} + 2 = 13$

5. One week for lunch, Jeff bought hamburgers for $5.25 each. He also bought a chicken sandwich for $5. He spent $26 in all. How many hamburgers did Jeff buy?

_____

i. $5x + 5.25 = 26$

j. $\dfrac{x}{5.25} - 5 = 26$

6. WRITE Math ▶ Choose one of the equations you did not use. Write a word problem that could be solved by using that equation. Solve your problem.

_____

_____

_____

Name _____

Crack the Sequence Code

Your mission: You've been hired by a top-secret agency to figure out the following codes of a rival agency. Find the missing terms of each code and write a rule for the sequence.

1. Item: **Secret Password**

38, 31, 62, 55, 110, _____, _____

Pattern: _____

2. Item: **Directions to Hideout**
4 miles north, 10 miles east, 25 miles

south, 62.5 miles west, _____,

_____,

Pattern: _____

_____

3. Item: **Number of Agents**
6 Level A Agents, 10 Level C Agents,

18 Level E Agents, _____,

_____, 130 Level K Agents

Pattern: _____

_____

4. Item: **Combination to the Safe**
9 turns to the right, 3 turns to the left,

1 turn to the right, _____,

_____, $\frac{1}{27}$ turn to the left

Pattern: _____

_____

5. Item: **Location of Secret Passageway**
Up two stairs, down one stair, up four

stairs, down two stairs, up six stairs, down

three stairs, _____,

_____

Pattern: _____

_____

6. Item: **Miles of Underground Tunnels**
Tunnel A: $7\frac{1}{2}$, Tunnel B: $9\frac{3}{4}$,

Tunnel C: _____, Tunnel D: $14\frac{1}{4}$,

Tunnel E: _____, Tunnel F: _____

Pattern: _____

_____

7. Stretch Your Thinking Now create a pattern for your own top-secret agency. Leave two terms blank in your code. Then write the rule for your pattern.

_____

_____

8. **WRITE Math** What steps did you use to create your pattern? Explain how you would find the two missing terms in your code.

_____

_____

© Houghton Mifflin Harcourt Publishing Company

Cellular Phone Functions

Josie is deciding on a calling plan for her new cell phone.
She is given the four monthly calling plans below. Write an
equation to show the function for each plan.

Plan A

Minutes (m)	Monthly Charge (c)
1	$20.15
2	$20.30
3	$20.45
4	$20.60

Plan B

Minutes (m)	Monthly Charge (c)
5	$6.50
10	$8.00
15	$9.50
20	$11.00

Plan C

Minutes (m)	Monthly Charge (c)
10	$4.50
20	$9.00
30	$13.50
40	$18.00

Plan D

Minutes (m)	Monthly Charge (c)
20	$11.00
30	$16.50
40	$22.00
50	$27.50

Match each company below with their plan.

1. Company Xenon charges $0.45 per minute.

   Plan: _____

2. Pythagorean Cellular charges $20 per month and $0.15 per minute.

   Plan: _____

3. Aztec Phone charges $0.55 per minute.

   Plan: _____

4. Triangular Wireless charges $0.30 per minute and a monthly $5 satellite fee.

   Plan: _____

5. **Stretch Your Thinking** Josie talks on the phone for an average of 50 minutes per month. Which plan is the cheapest for Josie?

6. **WRITE Math** Explain how to find which company has the cheapest plan.

Coordinate Grid Graphing Riddle

Graph each of the ordered pairs on the coordinate grid below. Then connect points 1–14 in the order that you plotted them to answer the riddle.

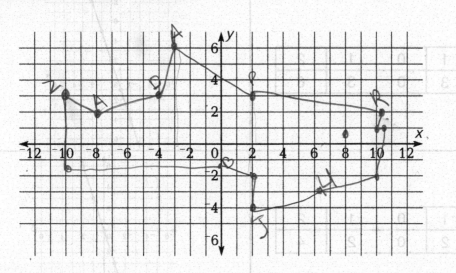

1. Z (⁻10, 3)	2. A (⁻8, 2)	3. D (⁻4, 3)
4. A (⁻3, 6)	5. P (2, 3)	6. R (9, 2)
7. C (10, 1)	8. K (9, ⁻1)	9. S (10, ⁻2)
10. H (5, ⁻3)	11. J (2, ⁻4)	12. A (2, ⁻2)
13. B (⁻8, ⁻1)	14. R (⁻10, ⁻3)	15. K (8, 1) (This is a separate point.)

Riddle: What animal can you see at the bottom of the ocean?

shark !)

Hint: After you've connected points 1–14, take the letters from the question numbers that are multiples of either 2 or 3 to spell out the answer.

What's My Line?

Draw a line that connects each table to the correct graph.

x	-2	-1	0	1	2
y	-6	-3	0	3	6

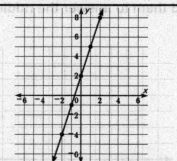

x	-2	-1	0	1	2
y	-4	-2	0	2	4

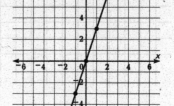

x	-2	-1	0	1	2
y	-4	-1	2	5	8

x	-2	-1	0	1	2
y	-2	-1	0	1	2

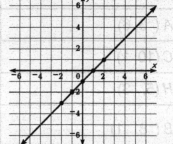

x	-2	-1	0	1	2
y	-3	-2	-1	0	1

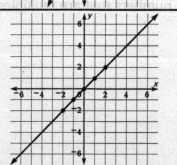

What's My Equation?

Circle the letter of the correct equation for each graph.

1.
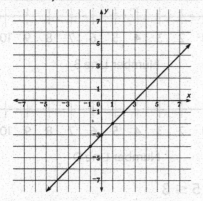

A $y = x + 3$ **C** $y = x - 3$

B $y = {}^-x + 3$ **D** $y = {}^-x - 3$

2.
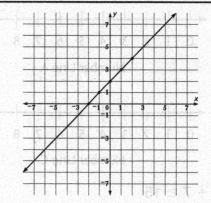

A $y = x + 2$ **C** $y = x - 2$

B $y = {}^-x + 2$ **D** $y = {}^-x - 2$

3.
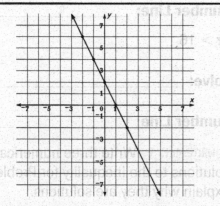

A $y = 2x + 2$ **C** $y = 2x - 2$

B $y = {}^-2x + 2$ **D** $y = {}^-2x - 2$

4.
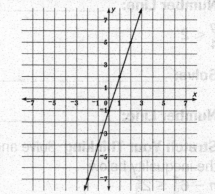

A $y = 3x + 1$ **C** $y = 3x - 1$

B $y = {}^-3x + 1$ **D** $y = {}^-3x - 1$

5.
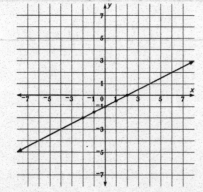

A $y = \frac{1}{2}x + 1$ **C** $y = \frac{1}{2}x - 1$

B $y = \frac{1}{2}x + 2$ **D** $y = \frac{1}{2}x - 2$

6.
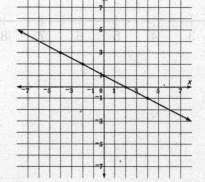

A $y = \frac{-1}{2}x + 1$ **C** $y = \frac{-1}{2}x - 1$

B $y = \frac{-1}{2}x + 2$ **D** $y = \frac{-1}{2}x - 2$

Inequalities on the Number Line

Solve the inequality. Match the inequality with the correct number line.

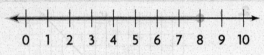

Number Line A

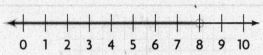

Number Line B

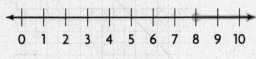

Number Line C

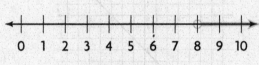

Number Line D

1. $y + 7 \geq 15$

Solve: _____

Number Line: _____

2. $h - 5 \leq 3$

Solve: _____

Number Line: _____

3. $\dfrac{g}{4} < 2$

Solve: _____

Number Line: _____

4. $2z > 16$

Solve: _____

Number Line: _____

5. Stretch Your Thinking Solve and graph the inequality below.

$n - 6\frac{1}{9} \leq 2\frac{2}{3}$

6. ⬛ **WRITE Math** ▸ Write three numerical solutions to the inequality for Problem 5. Explain why they are solutions.

_____

_____

_____

_____

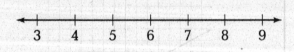

Name _____

Name and Classify the Angles

Name and classify the angles to the right.

1. Name and classify the angle that measures 135º.

_____

2. Name and classify the angle that measures 180º.

_____

3. Name and classify the angle that measures 20º.

_____

4. Name and classify the angle that measures 90º.

_____

5. Name and classify the angle that measures 75º.

_____

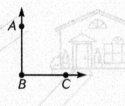
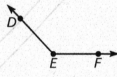
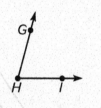
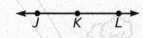
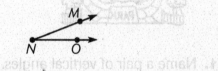

6. Stretch Your Thinking Draw an angle below that measures 160º. Name and classify the angle.

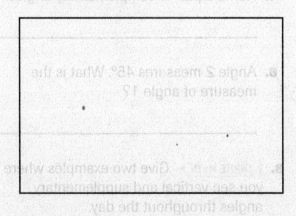

7. **WRITE Math** Explain how to draw a right angle without using a protractor.

_____

_____

_____

_____

_____

Welcome to Angleville

Use the map of Angleville to answer the questions.

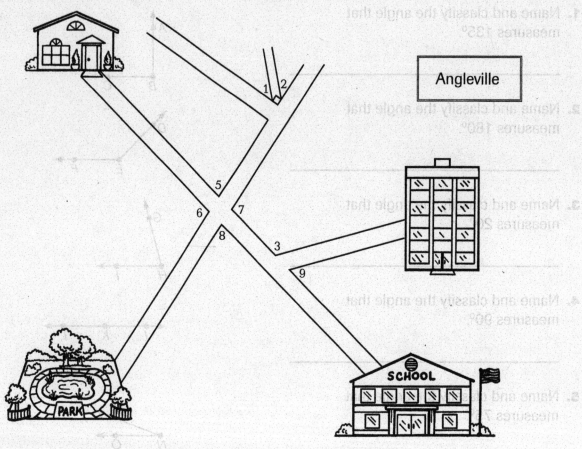

1. Name a pair of vertical angles.

2. Name a pair of supplementary angles.

_____

_____

3. Name a pair of adjacent angles.

4. Name a pair of complementary angles.

_____

_____

5. Angle 9 measures 63°. What is the measure of angle 3?

6. Angle 2 measures 45°. What is the measure of angle 1?

_____

_____

7. Stretch Your Thinking Angle 6 measures 98°. Find the measures of the following angles:

8. ⬛ WRITE Math ▸ Give two examples where you see vertical and supplementary angles throughout the day.

Angle 5: _____ Angle 7: _____

_____

This Is Your Life!

Polly Polygon is on a game show where each friend describes himself or herself. Use the clues to help Polly identify the friend. Write the name and the type of polygon and tell if it is regular or irregular.

1. I have four angles and they are all right angles. My opposite sides are congruent, but they are not all equal in length.

   Who am I? _____ , _____

   Regular or irregular? _____

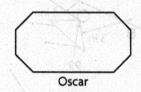
Oscar

2. Two of my angles measure 135°. I have six more angles. Not all of my sides are congruent.

   Who am I? _____ , _____

   Regular or irregular? _____

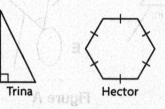
Trina   Hector

3. Two of my sides are congruent. So are two of my angles. My third side is shorter than the other two.

   Who am I? _____ , _____

   Regular or irregular? _____

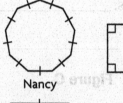
Nancy

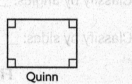
Quinn

4. I have more than four angles. I have an even number of sides. My angles are congruent.

   Who am I? _____ , _____

   Regular or irregular? _____

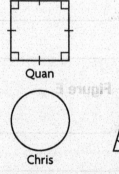
Quan

Chris

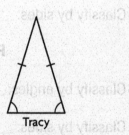
Tracy

5. **Stretch Your Thinking** Name and write a description of one of the polygons above that you didn't use.

   _____

   _____

   _____

   _____

6. **WRITE Math** Which of the figures above is not a polygon? Explain your answer.

   _____

   _____

   _____

   _____

Triangle Art Show

The figures below are pieces in an art show. Classify each triangle by its sides and angles.

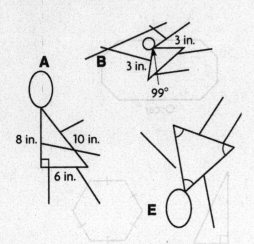 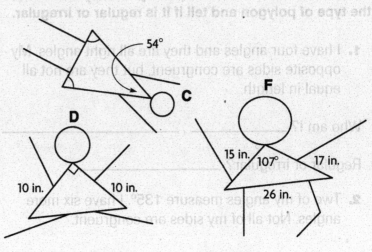

Figure A	**Figure B**
Classify by angles: _____	Classify by angles: _____
Classify by sides: _____	Classify by sides: _____
Figure C	**Figure D**
Classify by angles: _____	Classify by angles: _____
Classify by sides: _____	Classify by sides: _____
Figure E	**Figure F**
Classify by angles: _____	Classify by angles: _____
Classify by sides: _____	Classify by sides: _____

1. **Stretch Your Thinking** Draw an acute triangle that is a scalene triangle. Label the angles.

2. **WRITE Math** Can a triangle be an equilateral triangle and either obtuse or right? Explain your answer.

_____

_____

_____

_____

Who am I?

The four figures below are describing to you what they look like. Write
which type of quadrilaterals they are and draw pictures of them based on
their descriptions. Be sure to mark congruent sides and angles in the picture.

Ricardo	Trudy
I am a quadrilateral whose opposite sides are congruent and parallel. All my angles measure 90°. Two of my sides are not congruent to my other two sides. **1.** My name is Ricardo _____	I am a quadrilateral with two opposite sides that are parallel. Sometimes, two of my angles are congruent, but sometimes they're not. **2.** My name is Trudy _____
Ralph	**Sue**
I am a quadrilateral whose sides are all congruent to each other. My angles are congruent in pairs, but they don't have to be a certain measure. My opposite sides are parallel to each other. **3.** My name is Ralph _____	Ralph is my brother. I'm just like him except my angles each measure 90°. **4.** My name is Sue _____

5. Stretch Your Thinking Write a
description and draw a picture of Paul
the Parallelogram.

_____

_____

_____

6. WRITE Math ▸ A parallelogram has three
angles that measure 111°, 69°, and
111°. Explain how you would find the
measure of the other angle.

_____

_____

_____

_____

Angle Measures in Regular Polygons

Draw a diagram and use what you know about the angles of a regular polygon to solve each problem.

1. What is the measure of each angle of a regular pentagon? (Hint: Find the sum of the angle measures. Then use what you know about the angles of a regular polygon to find the measure of each angle.)

_____

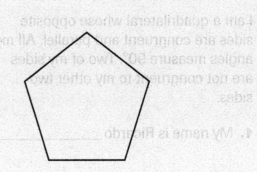

2. What is the measure of each angle of a regular hexagon?

_____

3. What is the measure of each angle of a regular octagon?

_____

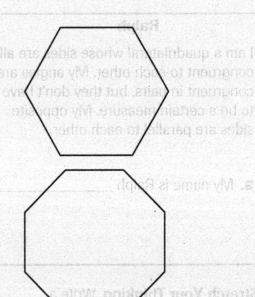

4. What is the measure of each angle of a regular 24-sided polygon?

_____

5. **Stretch Your Thinking** Write an expression for the sum of the measures of the angles of a regular polygon that has *n* sides. Then write an expression for the measure of each angle.

_____

_____

Hidden Picture

Use the clues to find the missing vertices. Plot the missing vertices on the coordinate grid and draw each quadrilateral to complete the picture below.

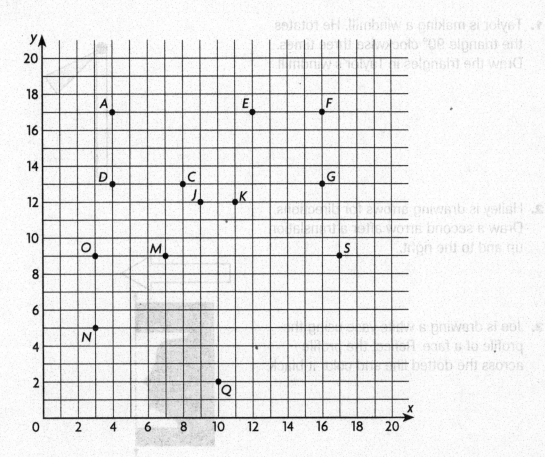

CLUES:

1. *ABCD* is a rectangle.

2. *EFGH* is a square.

3. *JKLM* is a trapezoid, and $\overline{LM}$ is 6 units long

4. *NOPQ* and *PQRS* are parallelograms.

Point *B*: _____

Point *H*: _____

Point *L*: _____

Point *P*: _____

Point *R*: _____

Transformations in Everyday Situations

Perform the transformations to make the objects.

1. Taylor is making a windmill. He rotates the triangle 90° clockwise three times. Draw the triangles in Taylor's windmill.

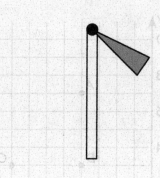

2. Hailey is drawing arrows for directions. Draw a second arrow after a translation up and to the right.

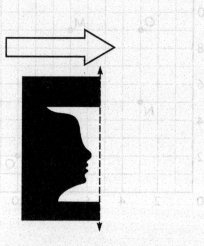

3. Joe is drawing a white vase using the profile of a face. Reflect the profile across the dotted line and color it black.

4. Stretch Your Thinking Tell what transformation was made to transform the figure to its next position.

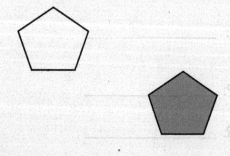

5. `WRITE Math` Transformations can change a figure's orientation (direction), location, and even its size. Which of the three characteristics change after a figure has been reflected? Explain how.

_____

_____

_____

_____

Symmetry You've Just Got to See

Complete the other half of the symmetrical figure. Use the figures to answer the questions.

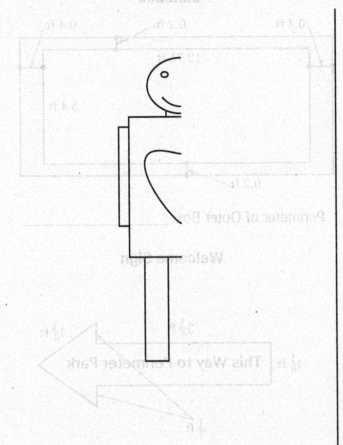

1.

Do the figures have any lines of symmetry? If so, how many?

_____

_____

2. Draw the lines of symmetry, if any, for the figures.

3. Do the figures have rotational symmetry?

_____

_____

4. If so, identify the symmetry for each as a fraction of a turn and in degrees.

_____

5. **Stretch Your Thinking** A palindrome is a word that is read the same forward and backward. You could say that it is symmetrical. Draw the lines of symmetry in the palindromes. Then write your own palindrome.

| KAYAK | ANNA |

_____

_____

6. ▐WRITE Math▐ Can a figure have rotational symmetry but not line symmetry? Explain.

_____

_____

Park Perimeters

Find the perimeters of the designs for objects at the park.

Seesaw

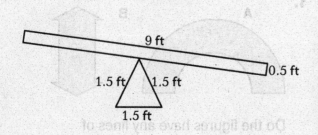

Total Perimeter: _____

Sandbox

Perimeter of Outer Box: _____

Slide

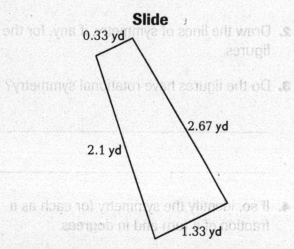

Total Perimeter: _____

Welcome Sign

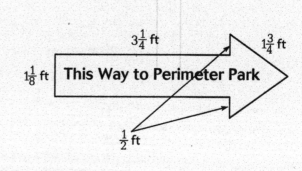

Perimeter of Sign: _____

1. Stretch Your Thinking The length and width of the sandbox has been doubled. How does this affect the perimeter?

_____

_____

_____

_____

2. **WRITE Math** If you are given the perimeter and lengths of 5 sides of a 6-sided figure, do you have enough information to find the length of the sixth side? Explain.

_____

_____

_____

_____

_____

Estimate Circumference to Find the Right Parts

Motors need the following parts. Estimate the circumferences of the circles below and choose the correct part for each motor.

1. A belt in a motor has a circumference of about 18 centimeters. Part: _____	**2.** A gear in a motor has a circumference of about 9 cm. Part: _____
3. A circular disc in a motor has a circumference of about 25 cm. Part: _____	**4.** A socket in a motor has a circumference of about $\frac{3}{4}$ cm. Part: _____
5. Another gear has a circumference of about 3 cm. Part: _____	**6.** A second belt has a circumference of about 56 cm. Part: _____

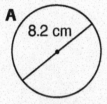
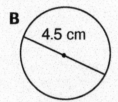
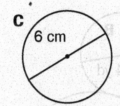
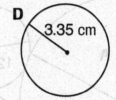
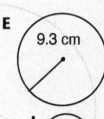

A 8.2 cm B 4.5 cm C 6 cm D 3.35 cm E 9.3 cm

F 3 cm G $1\frac{1}{2}$ cm H $\frac{1}{2}$ cm I $\frac{1}{4}$ cm J $\frac{1}{4}$ cm

7. Stretch Your Thinking Write a description for one of the two circles above that you did not choose. Include an estimate of the circumference.

_____

_____

_____

_____

8. **WRITE Math** Explain how to estimate the circumference of a circle when you're given the radius.

_____

_____

_____

_____

Circle Circumference Exercise Course

Ms. Connors created an exercise course for her gym class using
circles. Use the information to find the distances that students
jumped and ran to the nearest whole number of units.

Circle A	Circle B
Students warmed up by jogging around Circle A.	Students then ran twice around Circle B.
Distance: _____	Distance: _____

Circle C	Circles D and E
Students ran across the diameter of Circle C. The circumference of Circle C ≈ 62.83 yd.	Students jumped around Circles D and E. Both circles have the same diameter.
Distance: _____	Distance: _____

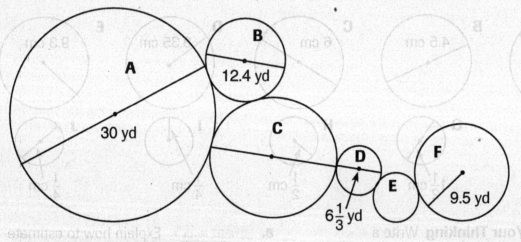

1. **Stretch Your Thinking** Students cooled
   down from the exercise course by walking
   $1\frac{1}{2}$ times around Circle F. Using your
   answers above, write the total distance of
   the course to the nearest whole number.

   _____

   _____

   _____

2. WRITE Math ▶ Explain how circumference
   and perimeter are alike.

   _____

   _____

   _____

   _____

   _____

Name _____

All Aboard Rectangle and Parallelogram Express

Find the areas of the train cars below. Write the shape of the car and the formula you used to find the area. (Do not include the wheels as part of the area.)

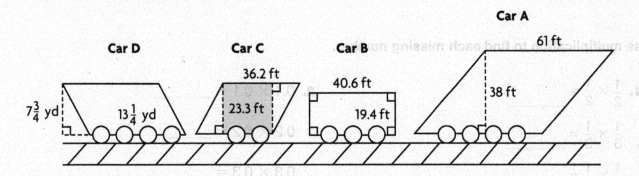

Train Car A	Train Car B
Figure: _____	Figure: _____
Formula for the Area: _____	Formula for the Area: _____
Area: _____	Area: _____
Train Car C	**Train Car D**
Figure: _____	Figure: _____
Formula for the Area: _____	Formula for the Area: _____
Area: _____	Area: _____

1. Stretch Your Thinking Add another car to the train. Draw and label the car. Then find the area.

2. Stretch Your Thinking If the unshaded triangles in Train Car C are removed, the figure is a square. What is the area of the shaded section of Train Car C?

_____   _____

Decimals and Fractions Squared

The square root of a number can be a decimal or a fraction. For example:

$$2\frac{1}{2} \times 2\frac{1}{2} = 6\frac{1}{4} \text{ so } \sqrt{6\frac{1}{4}} = 2\frac{1}{2}$$

$$4.6 \times 4.6 = 21.16, \text{ so } \sqrt{21.16} = 4.6$$

Use multiplication to find each missing number.

1. $\dfrac{1}{2} \times \dfrac{1}{2} =$ _____

$\dfrac{1}{3} \times \dfrac{1}{3} =$ _____

$\dfrac{1}{4} \times \dfrac{1}{4} =$ _____

$\dfrac{1}{5} \times \dfrac{1}{5} =$ _____

2. $0.1 \times 0.1 =$ _____

$0.2 \times 0.2 =$ _____

$0.3 \times 0.3 =$ _____

$0.4 \times 0.4 =$ _____

Use your answers to Exercises 1 and 2 and patterns to find each missing number.

3. $\left(\dfrac{1}{3}\right)^2 =$ _____

4. $\left(\dfrac{1}{9}\right)^2 =$ _____

5. $(0.4)^2 =$ _____

6. $(0.8)^2 =$ _____

7. $\sqrt{\dfrac{1}{25}} =$ _____

8. $\sqrt{\dfrac{1}{100}} =$ _____

9. $\sqrt{0.09} =$ _____

10. $\sqrt{0.49} =$ _____

11. ⟩WRITE Math⟩ What patterns do you see in the squares of unit fractions? Explain.

_____

_____

_____

_____

_____

Name _____

Tricky Triangles and Trapezoids

**Find the missing base or height of each triangle or trapezoid.
Write your answer in the box provided.**

1. $A = 21$ cm²

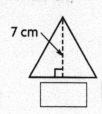

7 cm

2. $A = 125$ ft²

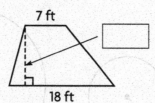

7 ft

18 ft

3. $A = 5$ cm²

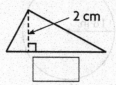

2 cm

4. $A = 120$ cm²

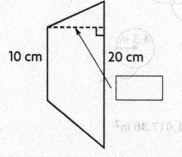

10 cm   20 cm

5. $A = 15$ in.²

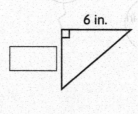

6 in.

6. $A = 240$ ft²

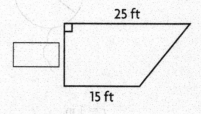

25 ft

15 ft

7. $A = 24$ mi²

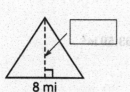

8 mi

8. $A = 88$ yd²

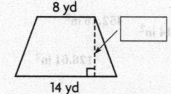

8 yd

14 yd

9. $A = 120$ km²

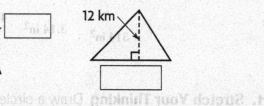

12 km

10. Stretch Your Thinking How can you change the base and height of the triangle in Exercise 7 so that the area remains the same?

_____

_____

_____

11. ⬛ **WRITE Math** Tell how you find the missing height of a trapezoid. Use Exercise 4 as an example.

_____

_____

_____

_____

_____

Pi Party

Draw lines connecting the circular balloons with their appropriate areas. Use 3.14 for π. Areas have been rounded to the nearest hundredth of an inch.

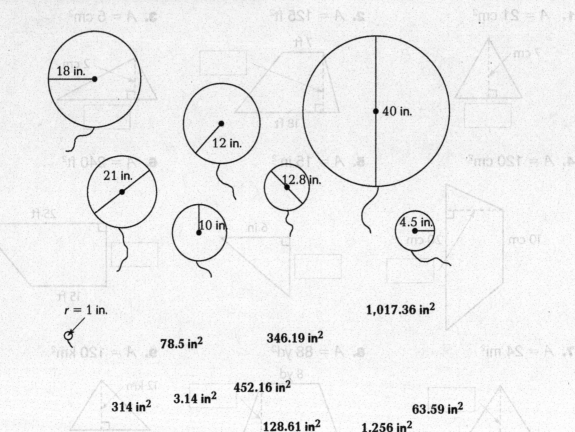

1. **Stretch Your Thinking** Draw a circle and label the radius so that the circle has an area to match the area that you did not use above.

2. **WRITE Math** Trevor found the area of a circle with a diameter of 16 yd. He squared the diameter and multiplied by 3.14. Since he used the diameter and not the radius, Trevor divided his answer by 2. Did Trevor make a mistake? Explain.

_____

_____

_____

_____

_____

Name _____

Circle Area Game

In this game, you are given pie pieces for questions you answer correctly. Answer each question on circle areas to fill your circular marker. Write answers to the nearest whole number of units. The "Your Marker" circle shows what your marker should look like if you got the previous questions correct.

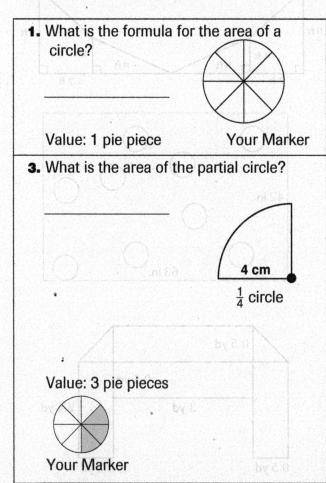

1. What is the formula for the area of a circle?

_____

Value: 1 pie piece   Your Marker

3. What is the area of the partial circle?

_____

4 cm

$\frac{1}{4}$ circle

Value: 3 pie pieces

Your Marker

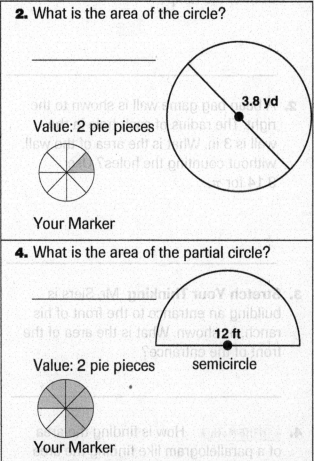

2. What is the area of the circle?

_____

3.8 yd

Value: 2 pie pieces

Your Marker

4. What is the area of the partial circle?

_____

12 ft

semicircle

Value: 2 pie pieces

Your Marker

5. Stretch Your Thinking If the radius of your marker is 3 cm, what is the area of the partial circle of your marker that was filled in before question 3?

_____

_____

6. [WRITE Math] Explain how you can find the area of $\frac{1}{3}$ of a circle if you know the circumference of the whole circle.

_____

_____

_____

Find Areas of Composite Figures

Solve.

1. A skateboard ramp is made of the figures as shown. What is the area of the front of the ramp?

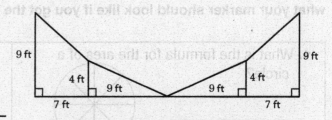

_____

2. A bean bag game wall is shown to the right. The radius of each hole in the wall is 3 in. What is the area of the wall, without counting the holes? Use 3.14 for π.

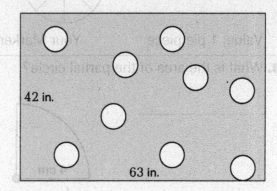

_____

3. **Stretch Your Thinking** Mr. Siers is building an entrance to the front of his ranch, as shown. What is the area of the front of the entrance?

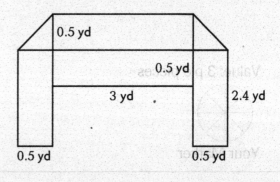

_____

4. **WRITE Math** How is finding the area of a parallelogram like finding the area of two congruent triangles? Explain your answer.

_____

_____

_____

_____

Fixing Perimeter and Area

You have explored how changing the dimensions of a polygon affects the perimeter and area. Now you will explore what happens when you fix the perimeter or area and allow the other measurements to change.

1. Complete the table to find the dimensions of the rectangle with the greatest area whose perimeter is 20 cm.

_____

Length (cm)	Width (cm)	Perimeter (cm)	Area (cm²)
9	1	20	9
8	2	20	
7			
6			
5			
4			
3			
2			
1			

2. Complete the table to find the dimensions of the rectangle with the least perimeter whose area is 36 cm².

_____

Length (cm)	Width (cm)	Perimeter (cm)	Area (cm²)
1	36	74	36
2	18		36
3			
4			
6			
9			
12			
18			
36			

3. Stretch Your Thinking What can you conclude about the dimensions of a rectangle with a fixed perimeter?

_____

_____

_____

4. Stretch Your Thinking What can you conclude about the dimensions of a rectangle with a fixed area?

_____

_____

_____

Name _____

Solid Identification

Use the figures below to answer the questions.

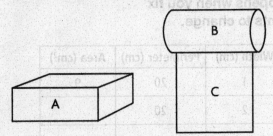
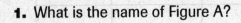
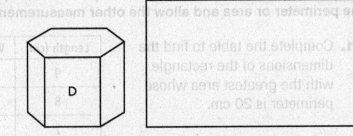

1. What is the name of Figure A?

_____

Is it a solid figure?

_____

If applicable, how many faces, edges, vertices and bases does the figure have?

_____

2. What is the name of Figure B?

_____

Is it a solid figure?

_____

If applicable, how many faces, edges, vertices and bases does the figure have?

_____

3. What is the name of Figure C?

_____

Is it a solid figure?

_____

If applicable, how many faces, edges, vertices and bases does the figure have?

_____

4. What is the name of Figure D?

_____

Is it a solid figure?

_____

If applicable, how many faces, edges, vertices and bases does the figure have?

_____

5. Stretch Your Thinking Draw a triangular prism in the rectangle at the top of the page.

If applicable, how many faces, edges, vertices and bases does the figure have?

_____

_____

6. **WRITE Math** Describe the similarities and differences between a pyramid and a cone.

_____

_____

_____

_____

Use Surface Area to Make Food Labels

You've been hired to design labels for the following food items. Each label will cover the entire package, including hidden surfaces. Match each item with its description. Then find the surface area to determine how much material you will need for each label. Use 3.14 for pi.

Item: Green Raptor Energy Drink	**Item: Country Cabin Corn**
The energy drink is an aluminum can with height 5 in. and radius 1 in. Item: _____ Surface Area: _____	The tin can has height 11 cm and radius 4 cm. Item: _____ Surface Area: _____
Item: Tasty Flakes and Raisins Cereal	**Item: Crystal Clear Spring Water**
The cereal box has length 10 in., width 2.5 in., and height 12.3 in. Item: _____ Surface Area: _____	The plastic bottle is made of two cylinders. The bottom cylinder has height 18 cm and radius 3 cm. The top cylinder has height 3 cm and radius 1 cm. Item: _____ Surface Area: _____

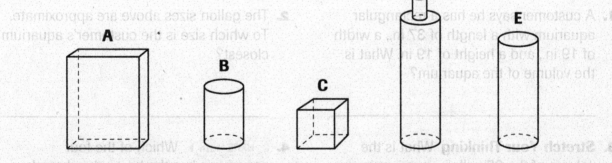

1. **Stretch Your Thinking** Paint and ink to cover the energy drink can costs $0.01 per square inch. How much money would it cost to cover six cans, to the nearest penny?

_____

_____

_____

2. **WRITE Math** Country Cabin decided they don't want a label on the top and bottom of the can. Using the surface area you found, explain how to find the new surface area.

_____

_____

_____

Aquarium Volumes on Display

A pet store is selling aquariums. You have been asked to find the volumes of the aquariums in cubic inches. After finding the volumes, answer the questions that follow.

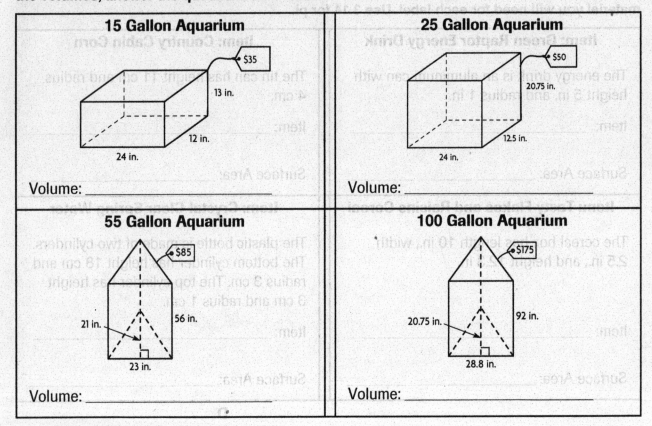

15 Gallon Aquarium
$35

13 in.
12 in.
24 in.

Volume: _____

25 Gallon Aquarium
$50

20.75 in.
12.5 in.
24 in.

Volume: _____

55 Gallon Aquarium
$85

21 in.   56 in.
23 in.

Volume: _____

100 Gallon Aquarium
$175

20.75 in.   92 in.
28.8 in.

Volume: _____

1. A customer says he has a rectangular aquarium with a length of 37 in., a width of 19 in., and a height of 19 in. What is the volume of the aquarium?

_____

2. The gallon sizes above are approximate. To which size is the customer's aquarium closest?

_____

3. Stretch Your Thinking What is the volume of the 25 gallon aquarium in *cubic feet*? Round to the nearest tenth.

_____

_____

_____

4. **WRITE Math** Which of the four aquariums has the best value, based on the advertised gallon sizes? Explain your answer.

_____

_____

_____

Volumes of Air Tubes

Some companies use a pneumatic tube system to transport money or documents within a building. A cylindrical tube filled with items is inserted into a tube system. Compressed air or a vacuum sends the tube to another room. Find the volume of each tube to the nearest whole number.

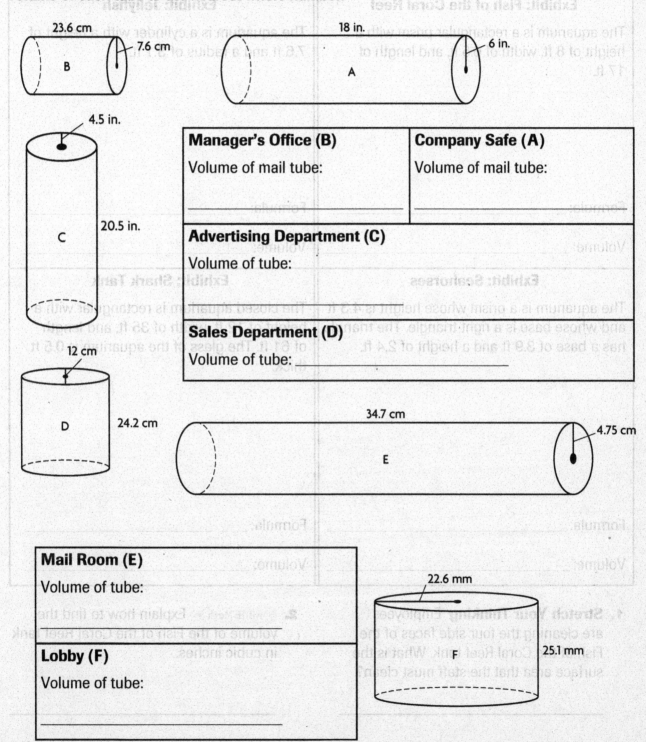

Manager's Office (B)

Volume of mail tube:

_____

Company Safe (A)

Volume of mail tube:

_____

Advertising Department (C)

Volume of tube:

Sales Department (D)

Volume of tube: _____

Mail Room (E)

Volume of tube:

Lobby (F)

Volume of tube:

_____

Volume at the Aquarium

The County Aquarium has four new exhibits. Draw and label
each exhibit and write the formula needed to find the volume
of water each aquarium can hold. Use the formula to find the
volume to the nearest whole number.

Exhibit: Fish of the Coral Reef	Exhibit: Jellyfish
The aquarium is a rectangular prism with a height of 8 ft, width of 6.5 ft, and length of 17 ft.	The aquarium is a cylinder with a height of 7.6 ft and a radius of 3.1 ft.
Formula: _____	Formula: _____
Volume: _____	Volume: _____
Exhibit: Seahorses	**Exhibit: Shark Tank**
The aquarium is a prism whose height is 4.3 ft and whose base is a right triangle. The triangle has a base of 3.9 ft and a height of 2.4 ft.	The closed aquarium is rectangular with a height of 12 ft, width of 35 ft, and length of 61 ft. The glass of the aquarium is 0.5 ft thick.
Formula: _____	Formula: _____
Volume: _____	Volume: _____

1. **Stretch Your Thinking** Employees are cleaning the four side faces of the Fish of the Coral Reef tank. What is the surface area that the staff must clean?

_____

_____

2. **WRITE Math** Explain how to find the volume of the Fish of the Coral Reef tank in cubic inches.

_____

_____